# SEPTEMBER MORNING:

# SEPTEMBER MORNING:
## A Practical Guide to the Middle Years

**Mildred Tengbom**

BRETHREN PRESS
Elgin, Illinois

September Morning: A Practical Guide to the Middle Years

BRETHREN PRESS, 1451 Dundee Avenue, Elgin, IL 60120

Cover design by Kathy Kline

Portions of this book were previously published as *The Bonus Years*, Augsburg Publishing House, 1975.

Unless otherwise noted, scriptural quotations are from the *Revised Standard Version of the Bible*, copyright 1946, 1952, 1971, and 1977 by the Division of Christian Education, National Council of Churches.

**Library of Congress Cataloging in Publication Data**

Tengbom, Mildred.
    September morning.

    1. Middle age.   2. Conduct of life.   I. Title.
HQ1059.4.T46   1985          305.2'44          85-19035
ISBN 0-87178-776-8

Printed in the United States of America

# Acknowledgements

Thank you:
> to the many who worked with me in group discussions
> to those who answered questionnaires
> to those whose stories are contained in this book
> to those who read and critiqued portions or all of the book
> to my husband, Luverne, and to our children, Dan, Judy, Barry, Janet, David and Becky who constantly encourage and cheer me on, as well as certain special friends
> and, most of all, to my Lord and Savior, Jesus Christ, who gave himself to redeem me and who has made and continues to make life beautiful for me.

# Contents

Preface: September Morning ix

1. Sensing a Nip in the Air 1
2. Oh, Those Aching Bones! 11
3. Early Frost: Disabilities 33
4. Driving on Rain-Slicked Roads: High Level Tension 43
5. Fall's Foggy Days as Marriage Sags 57
6. School Begins: Steps That Lead Away From Home 77
7. The Last Harvest: Caring for Aging Parents 93
8. Trees That Stand Alone 109
9. Will We Have Enough Stored Up for Winter? 127
10. Can I Learn to Ski and Skate at My Age? 141
11. Special Demands of Autumn and Winter 159
12. Keeping Green As Autumn Fades 173
13. Charting My Course: Setting Goals 179

# Preface:

# September Morning

The crisp, cool September morning reddened my nose and caused me to quicken my step as I strode down the path in the park. Spring and summer lay behind; fall and winter stretched ahead.

Spring had been chilly, delayng the fresh green budding of trees and the flowering of snow-white crocuses and vibrant red and yellow tulips. Sunny days, however, had relieved the grey ones.

Summer had sped by quickly in spite of torrid, sticky days that had shortened tempers, drained one's energy and triggered sudden violent and frightening thunder storms. Fortunately, pleasant, temperate days and nights of gentle rain had broken the cycle from time to time bringing welcome change and relief.

Now autumn and winter lay ahead. I wondered as I crossed the little bridge over a stream what those months would bring. Was not autumn a time to prepare for winter? I asked myself.

As a child in rural Minnesota I had understood the significance of changing seasons. I had watched mother fill the shelves with fruit and vegetables, pickles and relish, preserved from the garden and orchard she had nourished through spring and summer. I had helped father harvest grain, potatoes, hay and corn. I had carried afternoon coffee to him in the woods when he was felling and splitting wood to burn in our furnace throughout the long winter months. I had helped mother wash windows as we hung the storm windows to insulate against winter's penetrating cold blasts. Autumn during my childhood had been a time of preparation, a time of getting ready for the inescapable winter that lay ahead.

Winter had its own special gifts, such as extended hours of darkness allowing us more time to sleep. There was cold weather and blizzards which shut us in. These times permitted us to enjoy dominoes and checkers and puzzles in between chores because there was little else that we could do. Winter, accompanied by festive Thanksgiving and Christmas celebrations, brought families and neighbors together. True enough, winter also ushered in problems, but we didn't fear the season. We prepared for it, and autumn was the time to do a major part of that preparation.

I roused myself from my reverie. I was no longer a child. I was an adult now, poised midway through life. Was it not September for me in a new way now? And did not this mean that the time stretching immediately would have its most significance as I used it to prepare for the inescapable winter of life that lay ahead?

Would not how I used these next years determine to a large extent the quality of the final years of life and what those years would hold? Several areas of concern surfaced, especially with regard to health, an ability to relax and enjoy life, the courage to face declining strength and disabilities, and marital happiness. Would I enjoy good relationships with our children and aging parents, a strong sense of security, a caring support system, a continuing enthusiasm for life and an eagerness to learn, and a willingness to continue to live and act responsibly?

I drew a deep breath and quickened my pace. How could I chart a clear and sure course through the busy autumn ahead so winter would find me enriched, vibrantly alive, rejoicing in our Lord, and looking forward to a new, eternal spring?

Such reflection on the opportunities and problems of mid-life led to the publication of *The Bonus Years* in 1975. It was based on personal experiences, extensive reading, research in small groups of people in various churches, and questionnaires which were sent to about 80 people. The book was welcomed by many as a helpful guide to dealing with midlife stress, as well as joys.

Numerous changes in attitudes toward middle age have taken place within the past ten years. American society is more affluent, although problems brought about by rapid inflation have become the concern of many. Health issues have almost become a national past time. The first post-World War II "baby boomers" are now turning forty. Divorce and single parenting are more common than ever. Some in midlife find their children returning home, perhaps with grandchildren. Churches are searching for creative ways to be in ministry to those shaken by midlife tensions, as well as singles (of all ages) and those facing retirement. A practical resource for dealing with middle years seems as much needed as ever before.

I am thankful to the Brethren Press and its editors for their encouragement in revising the earlier book. *September Morning* is the result. The material has been completely reworked and includes updated statistics, suggestions for further reading, and new illustrations. The names of some persons have been changed or the surname withheld to protect their privacy, but all the stories are true.

Mildred Tengbom

# 1

## Sensing a Nip in the Air

*In the middle of the road of life I found myself in a dark wood having strayed from the straight path.*

*—Dante*

"I was running, running, running," David Rothschild said. "Running because I was afraid to slow down to think. I feared I might discern my goals were not as meaningful as I, a successful real estate broker, had thought."

In midlife the questions already were there in David's heart, crying for an answer. But he kept pushing them back, becoming busier and busier, so he would not have time to think.

### Not an Uncommon Experience

It happens to almost all men, usually between the ages of 39 and 42—and sometimes later—according to Yale psychologist, Daniel Levinson. He drew his conclusion after a three-year study of males, aged 35 to 45. Of course, important questions had been faced earlier, in adolescence. Now, in midlife men face questions again, but this time the issues differ from those they faced in adolescence. When young they asked: Who am I? Now they ask, Who have I been? As teenagers they asked, What is it worth? Now they ask, What is worthy? Middle aged men also differ from teenagers in that they have had an opportunity to test what they thought they believed in. However, both teenagers and middle-aged ask, Who will I continue to be?

Women, too, begin to face these questions in midlife. However, for women more than for men, a precise time when they begin to question their identity, values, and accomplishments may vary depending on different situations.

The questions for men and women continually probe: Who am I? Why was I born? What is the meaning of life? What have I accomplished? For what will I be remembered? What will happen to me after death? Has life been worth the hassle?

As children, sons and daughters, of a loving God, it is highly important that we find satisfying answers to key life questions. If we don't we shall not be able to move along to enjoy and satisfy the basic needs of our next span of life, the senior years, old age—winter—which lies immediately ahead.

For every age span in life has its own unique developmental tasks. Erik H. Erikson has defined them in several stages: (1) early infancy—trust; (2) later infancy—autonomy; (3) early childhood—initiative; (4) middle years of childhood—industry; (5) adolescence—career, sex role, and a system of values; (6) early adulthood—intimacy; (7) middle adulthood—generativity or expansion of interests and a sense of contributing to the future; (8) late adulthood—ego integrity or the basic acceptance of one's life as having been meaningful.

## A Second Chance

The middle years, or our September mornings, offer us if we need it, a second chance, a time to rethink and reorder our lives. It is a season in which we may begin to live differently, creatively. At the end of life we shall be able to look back with satisfaction and be ready to die with peace and serenity.

How did it work out for David Rothschild?

"I was running, running, afraid to stop and think," David said. "And then suddenly I was hauled up short in my pursuit of money, success, and pleasure, for my son, my only son, was in trouble.

"Hooked on methedrine. Shooting up with heroin, 'Tripping' with LSD. This had led to burglary, car theft, and heavy drinking. For five years I existed in a living hell. Three times, shame washing over me, I heard the judge commit my son to juvenile jail.

"To pay lawyers, doctors, and psychiatrists I had to work more frantically than ever. Yet all the time disturbing questions kept nudging me: Was this all there was to life? No more meaning than this? Troubles, sorrow, disappointments and then the grave?

"I began to drink. I planned exciting vacations. My wife and I filled our social calendar. I pushed the sale of more houses.

"My son's condition worsened. He was committed to a state hospital. When the doctors dismissed him, we were told that they could do nothing more for him, that we should never expect him to be a productive adult. I felt worse than ever. I didn't know where to turn. No matter what authority I had appealed to, none could give me hope. I wished life would end."

David ordered his son to find a job. The woman at the employment bureau referred the son to a woman who, she thought, could help him. He went to see her.

A short while later the phone in David's home jangled. It was his son. "I've prayed to receive Christ," he announced. "My sins are forgiven!"

"I thought he had really gone off the deep end," David confessed. "I hurried to the lady's house to rescue him. To my surprise the lady appeared to be sane, quiet, and pleasant."

David took his son home. Day after day David watched him. Something *had* happened. His son was different. No drugs. No strange behavior. A completely new attitude. David was dumbfounded. How could one little prayer to Jesus work such a miracle? David looked and looked at his son and wondered.

"The lady began to visit us," David recalled. "I listened as she explained the Bible, though not without conflict. My wife and I were practicing meditation at the time. I played one of our meditation records for the lady. She politely listened, and then talked about the Bible some more. My wife, a graduate of the University of Southern California, had majored in psychology. Her intellect told her that religious faith was just a crutch. But the lady continued to come and talk to us.

"About two weeks later alone in my home I prayed, not really expecting to be heard. 'Jesus,' I said, 'I am a sinner. Come into my heart and cleanse me of my sins.' The amazing thing was that after I had prayed, I knew it had happened. God had accepted me, forgiven me. The long, long search for inner peace and rest had come to an end. About six weeks later my wife committed herself to Christ.

"What an upheaval! Inner peace and joy replaced frustration and restless searching. Our whole set of values was turned upside down. Now Christ became of supreme importance, and then the spiritual welfare of others. Money, success, prestige, pleasure, all slid to the bottom of the list. Life suddenly became very meaningful and wonder-filled."

David's son, restored to full health, found employment, married, and became the proud father of a healthy, happy son. David sold his lucrative real estate business which demanded so much time from him and began to oversee a large apartment unit.

"In these units I found my field of ministry," David said. "How many are distressed, torn by family conflicts, coming apart as persons. I take care of my business with my clients first, and then I talk to them about One who loves them, who can help them as he helped me. Some listen. Some don't. And some have committed themselves to Christ."

### What Causes People to Re-evaluate?

A number of different things can cause people to re-evaluate the way they are living their lives. In David's case it was a family crisis. In some cases it may be being forced to come to terms with the fact that some of the dreams that had been cherished will never come to pass. Many things may contribute to what people perceive as failure. Why do dreams not come true?

In the first place, some dreams were too extravagant. Perhaps personalities hindered rather than enabled. Or maybe obstacles beyond control blocked progress: personal or family illness, accidents, financial problems, difficulties of employment. Whatever the cause, many begin to realize with a flat taste in their mouths that they have come as far as they can. Realizing that, they may begin to re-examine their original goals to ask if they really were as important as they had thought.

Oddly enough, however, success can also trigger questioning. John Killinger in his book *Christ in the Seasons of Ministry* refers to the pastor of a large, prestigious church, entering the last phase of his ministry. Killinger asked the pastor what thoughts ran through his mind and was surprised by the answer. "Sex and love," was the reply and went on to describe his struggle. He was attracted to many women, even to the point of lusting after intimate relationships with them.

Then he waved his arm to encompass the elaborate complex of buildings erected during his ministry. "I used to think the ultimate was to build all this," he said. "But now that it's built I think a lot about love. What good is a building if the people aren't changed? I'd like to spend the rest of my ministry teaching people how to love."

What a thought provoking combination of interests: sex and love captivated this man in midlife. Having stifled that most basic of all human needs, the need to love and be loved, and to help people to love, that need, so long ignored was now asserting itself in obsessive, distorted urges to have sex with any woman to whom he was attracted. And in struggling with these temptations the minister was discovering that success in what he had first thought to be all-important, a building program, really was not that significant.

Do women in midlife ask the same questions? This will vary, I think, depending on what the years up to this point have held for them.

For the single career woman, professionally successful by choice, but perhaps childless, midlife may present a unique crisis. While there always is time to marry, a woman's time to bear children is limited. Some single women find fulfillment outside of marriage and family in absorbing work and outside interests, perhaps in nurturing the children of others. But for many others being unmarried and childless becomes a painful issue as they ask what meaning life will hold for them in the future. Generally speaking, it has been found that women without children have much more difficulty perceiving their lives to be eminently worthwhile than do men who are successful in their chosen fields but are still childless. Birthdays, anniversaries, their own parent's wedding anniversaries, an invitation to the wedding of a peer who does marry late in life—all can accentuate the pain of an unmarried childless woman.

The woman who is a mother as well as a wife may react in varied ways to midlife. If her chief interest has been invested in her children, she may find it difficult, even impossible, to let them go. I was once a guest in a home where the rooms of the children told a sad story. The children now in their thirties and forties, were married and settled in homes with their own families. But their rooms in the parental home looked just as they must have looked when the children left to go to college. Pictures on the walls, trophies in the book case, pennants, stuffed animals on the beds, festive party hats perched on the top edges of mirrors were all the same.

A different situation arises when children have brought sorrow to their parents to the degree that the parents have despaired and felt life held no more meaning for them. Midlife suicides among such parents are not uncommon.

Some women, to alleviate financial pressures, work outside the home when the children enter school. Now that the children are grown and the family's financial situation more secure, they could quit their job but don't. Some do not want to give up the financial benefits that will continue to accrue. Others do not know how to invest free time and feel more useful and worthwhile while working at an outside job. And so they continue, neither particularly happy at their job nor happy when not working. Unfortunately, many never take the time nor make the effort to examine the cause of their vague discontent and restlessness.

On the other hand, some married women who have raised

their children respond joyously to the new-found freedom mid-life brings them. They begin to pursue either dreams long cherished or dreams newly awakened. These women may be so captivated by these fresh opportunities that they unconsciously may postpone the asking of serious questions until much later.

In some cases physical or behaviorial changes prompt persons to come to terms with midlife. We fall asleep in the chair at the end of the day. We note with disbelief someone else is making the overseas sales trip that we had been expecting to make. We have finally saved enough money to start our own business now but find ourselves scared to take that kind of risk. We accuse the cleaners of shrinking our clothes. We catch ourselves reading the obituary columns and comparing ages. We worry about minor physical ailments. It jars us when a younger classmate in a college course says, "I wish my mother would take some courses." We had been fooling ourselves into thinking that we were part of the crowd. After all, we can still do floor exercises with them. Again in college classes we find ourselves referring to books or plays or TV programs about which our classmates know nothing. We become edgy and critical of those who succeed. We feel our children aren't appreciating us. We preface our remarks with "when I was your age . . . " And we find ourselves focusing more on ourselves and our own needs than on our sons and daughters. A father may feel threatened by his son's size (particularly height) and feel that he still has to show in some way that he is boss. Both husband and wife increasingly take irritations of the day out on each other and on the family. Boredom can be oppressive. Marriage is old hat. We scrutinize ourselves in the mirror and fret about added pounds, wrinkles, paunches, thinning hair, brown spots and baldness. Yet with all of these painful observations we derive some small comfort from the fact that we are more thoughtful, and less judgmental because we are more unsure. At the same time that we explode we can also be very gentle. We despair, yet we are ever hopeful. All of these strange behaviors can cause us to admit finally to ourselves that we have arrived at a crisis point: we are middle-aged.

### The Problem Is More Than Middle Age

Just being middle-aged wouldn't be so bad. But what really disturbs us is that as we look ahead—which forever remains natural for us—we see something we like even less: aging and, eventually, death. To avoid this our thoughts and references tend to return to the past. Such returning to the past brings back memories of dreams cherished when we were young, many of them unrealized. And then the questions surface again.

"It takes courage to look back over one's life and re-evaluate," a successful business man said to me one day after we had been discussing the subject. Indeed it does. For one thing, we might see the need for change, and it always takes courage to change.

We need to bear in mind, however, that re-evaluation does not always involve change. It can also mean confirmation, a narrowing down, or a widening out.

But whatever the results are, it is imperative that the re-evaluation be done, that the questions be asked: Who have I been? Who will I be? What is worthy? The extent to which we answer these questions will determine, to an appreciable degree, the quality of the latter years of our lives. Life doesn't just happen. The future to some extent is something we create.

John W. Rilling recounts the story of Saint Philip Neri talking with a student at a university one day. The student's ambitions were great, and his talents forecast a successful career. The saint asked the student about his studies and his plans for the future.

"Right now I am studying philosophy," the student replied, "but I hope to graduate next year."

"And then?" queried the saint.

"Then I shall go on to study civil law and win my degree as a doctor."

"And then?"

"Then I shall become a lawyer and begin my practice."

"And then?"

"Then I expect I shall marry and settle down. I hope to have a family and probably will inherit the estate of my father."

"And then?"

"Why then I suppose I shall be satisfied with the position I have won, and shall be respected by my fellow citizens; and then like everybody else, shall grow old and die."

"And then?"

The young man hesitated. His lips began to quiver. Two little words, "And then?" had hauled him up short.

## A Second Chance

"What would you do?" another man asked, "if you felt you'd messed up your life?"

"I suppose I'd feel bad," I answered. "But I don't think I'd want to waste too much time on tears. I'd try to be thankful that life has not been lived in vain if I have now discovered what is truly important. I'd thank God for the forgiveness he offers me and then move on from there."

If we will let Christ take over our remaining years, with the guidance of the Holy Spirit, they will be beautiful, fulfilling years. God is able and wants to do this. It is comforting to remember that life is not only longevity. It also contains the qualities of breadth and depth and these often outweigh the influences of longevity. Jesus, after all, lived only 33 years.

Reflection and re-evaluation can be done at retreats or we can do it on our own. "Life was becoming so confusing and meaningless for me," a business executive said to me, "that I finally asked for a couple of days off. I drove out to a little rented cabin in the desert and there thought and prayed my way back to tranquility and purposefulness."

Prepared questions can be helpful as guide lines. Some will be included at the end of this chapter. But remember to let the Holy Spirit guide you. Be alert to hear the " . . . still, small voice." The Psalmist of old has put into words a prayer we can pray as we meditate: "Search me, O God, and know my heart! Try me, and know my thoughts! And see if there be any wicked way in me, and lead me in the way everlasting!" (Psalm 139:23-24.

## Questions for Discussion

You may want to answer the following questions for your own sake, or you may want to share the answers with your spouse or a friend. Be honest, candid, and open.

Complete the following:

1. When I was in high school I dreamed about . . .
2. Today when I think about this I . . .
3. As I look back over my life I feel good about . . .
4. What would I like to see different about me or life as it affects me?
5. What can I hope to accomplish in the remaining years of my life given my background, circumstances, talents, education, potentialities and in the light of my "track record" so far?
6. As I work toward the fulfillment of my goals how can I also savor the "now"?
7. As I consider my past life, how would I rate it? Explain.
   a. Very satisfying and rewarding.
   b. Satisfying, but I feel there must be something more.
   c. As good a life as most people have had so I should be satisfied, shouldn't I?
   d. What I've accomplished doesn't seem as important now as it did twenty years ago.
   e. I don't feel life has been worth all the hassle.
8. If I could control my future what do I wish it could contain for me?

Spend some time talking with the Lord about these things.

**2**

# Oh Those Aching Bones!

*Middle age is a time when you stop taking
your body for granted and start taking care
of it instead.*
                                    —Barbara Fried

If we are going to be able to fulfill the goals that we set for
our second half of life, we are going to need to be in as good
health as possible. Thus caring for our body and developing
buoyant mental health takes on added meaning. We are motivated to make called-for changes. Here are some suggestions:

**1. Stop self-diagnosing and pay attention to warning
signals.** Many of us have been used to diagnosing our own
ailments and prescribing treatment for them. Now, however, if
we are interested in assuring ourselves of good health during
the last half of our lives, we need to seek more intentionally the
help of those professionally trained.

Of course, the way in which we already have lived life to
this point will make a difference too. We can't mistreat our
bodies and thumb our nose at biological laws and then not expect to pay the price. If we ate rich foods in our 20s, we
deposited cholesterol and triglyceride plaques in our blood
vessels. By our 30s these plaques have striae through them; in
our 40s atherosclerosis is evident, and "the blood hangs in the
veins like silt."

But what's past is past. The damage done is done. The best thing that we can do is to take care of our bodies from now on. We ought not to play doctor any longer. Yet some of us stubbornly refuse to obtain competent medical advice because we were reared by magnificent parents and grandparents who cheerfully and stoically accepted aches and pains as part of the lot of wayward humans. This training was unfortunate, because ignoring an ache won't make it go away. Pain often is our kindest friend, alerting us to hidden trouble that will become only worse if ignored.

Also, the danger is greater for us in the middle years because the body sends back more subdued alarms than it did before. "Minor" complaints may be minor only in the sense or degree to which they are actually felt. For example, body temperature changes with age: a child's temperature may soar to 104 or 105 degrees. In a young adult it may be 102 or 103; in an older person it may not go higher than 100 or 101, and yet the infection may be as great or even greater. But because we are conditioned to think in terms of the higher temperatures of children, we refuse to regard lower temperatures as serious.

We need to understand also that remission of symptoms usually does not occur spontaneously. Disorders that are ignored do not disappear but usually get progressively worse. When the warning bell of aches and pains begins to ring, make an appointment with your doctor.

**2. Follow your doctor's orders.** Many of us have been inconsistent, even lazy, about actually following the doctor's orders. We listen carefully. Yet the diet recommended seems too restrictive, the exercise too difficult to fit into an already overcrowded schedule, the medication prescribed doesn't appear to be doing any good, so we often simply ignore the doctor's orders. Perhaps we may obey the instructions for a while, feel better, and then, because we do feel better, fail to follow through on our doctor's recommendations.

Again, we need to understand that effective control treatment requires (1) diagnosis of the disease early enough before irreparable damage has occurred, and (2) continuing close cooperation. You cannot treat disorders for a little while and then forget all about them just because the subjective symptoms have subsided, any more than you can navigate a ship by setting it upon a compass course and then ignoring it.

Changes in attitude toward health and diet and in response to warning signals are extremely important because the progression of many diseases may be arrested. These include: high blood pressure, gout, pernicious anemia, diabetes, thyroid inadequacy, even heart trouble. But we must assume responsibility for our own care. Only we can do it. Our physician should educate us and train us, then we must take over. In many cases it is possible to extend the years of our lives with proper diet and health care.

Mel Iverson's heart problems crept up on him slowly. When he was 53 he noticed his arms ached when he washed the car or mowed the lawn. One day his wife, Lydia, came home and found him resting after every swatch of lawn he cut. Shortly afterwards Mel was sitting in his office when he felt a heavy pressure in his chest. He walked across the street to his doctor's office, but the doctor had other patients and was unable to see him. Mel went back to his office. The pains increased. Finally when he was able to see the doctor, he had already had a heart attack. For six weeks he rested in the hospital, waiting for nature to repair some of the damage.

After that first attack Mel had to exercise constant vigilance. He carried nitroglycerine tablets and usually took only one a day, sometimes none, but during bad days he occasionally had to take three. Whenever any exertion caused the slightest pain, he stopped immediately, took a pill, and laid down to rest. On good days he could walk two miles, on bad days he could walk only two blocks. He swam but couldn't go in water deeper than five feet. "I don't like to wade with the kids," he confessed, "but I have no choice." He learned to accept his limitations and adapted. This allowed him to work twelve years after his heart attack until his retirement at 65, and he continued an active, full life until his death—partly accidental—at 75.

So serious health problems in the middle years need not mean a life of inactivity or invalidism. It often does mean a life where activities are curtailed to match the functional capacity of the body. It is not always a question of being prohibited from doing certain things we want to do, but a question of how we do them.

**3. Proper care of our bodies now may help insure health-ful years to come.** Changes in our attitude toward the care of our bodies is important also because the care we give ourselves during the middle years will affect in a positive way what our health will be like in our 60s and 70s. If we can reach 60 without one or more of the progressive disorders of old age, the outlook into the 80s is hopeful indeed. If the chronic progressive disorders are discovered early, there is plenty of time for treatment to accomplish much. The early diagnosis of high blood pressure, arthritis, or hardening of the arteries may be of little immediate concern, nor is a person likely to be disabled for a long time. Progression of disease can be slowed down if we are alert and obedient to our bodies' signals.

To maintain good health it is helpful for us to become informed about the most common ailments of aging and be able to recognize the early warning signals and know what to do. The following paragraphs discuss common medical concerns of life's September morning.

*Cardiac Concerns*

Increasingly, heart problems are becoming a concern of the middle years. Doctors warn that if those in midlife want to avoid cardiac disease, some important changes may be necessary if the person (1) uses tobacco, (2) is overweight, (3) gets little exercise, (4) lives and works under considerable stress. Medical experts agree that these are the four chief contributing factors toward making a person a likely candidate for heart problems of one kind or another.

George Rifa of Los Angeles had been a heavy smoker for 35 years and had tried to stop for 10. At 46 George met Christ, and his whole life, which he had succeeded quite well in messing up, was revolutionized. The slavery to smoking, however, continued for another two years. Suddenly one day in worship a word was spoken that struck him as a direct message from God that the day of liberation for him had come. He walked out of church and hasn't smoked since. For George, his freedom from tobacco was a miracle. For others, however, such sudden and dramatic miracles don't seem to happen. Perhaps Christians don't emphasize enough Christ's power to liberate us from harmful habits.

Fighting overweight has been a life-long problem for me, personally, demanding constant vigilance and discipline. I can remember sitting in the doctor's office when I was 18 and hearing him say: "You might as well make up your mind right now that you're never going to be able to eat as much as most other people without putting on weight." At 18 I wasn't ready to accept that. When midway through life I knew he was right.

It's not easy to maintain the proper weight in a wealthy, prosperous country. Magazine, TV, and radio advertising; restaurant menu delights; and supermarket displays all seem leagued in an all-out effort to make us fat. "Eat away," "stuff yourself," "enjoy the rich taste," they say. We have to learn to make faces at them.

A few lessons I have learned may help someone else.

1. I had to stop tearing myself down. If I didn't have a physical body like a fashion model, what other God-given gifts did I have which could be developed? When I gained weight, rather than hating myself for it, I learned to say, "Oh—oh! time to take things in hand again." The quicker I took off the excess pounds, the easier it was. I learned never to say, "I gained only two pounds; I don't worry about that." Multiply two by twenty years and what do I have? Forty pounds of excess! My kidneys and heart and liver have remained the same size, but now they have to do the work for a body-and-a-half. And, oh, my poor aching legs and back! Being overweight 25 percent above normal increases by 174 percent my chances of dying early; only 10 percent overweight increases my chance of an early death

by 20 percent—and I love to live.

2. I had to stop blaming others—and God—for my being overweight and accept responsibility for it myself. I grew up on a farm. Farmers work hard and burn up a lot of calories. Mother was a superb cook, and I just didn't realize that I didn't need all the food my brothers ate. Eating patterns were begun early. I had to learn that I could choose to change. If I were gaining weight, I was the only one making me that way. And if I were to take seriously Paul's admonition in Romans 12 to present my body to Christ as a living sacrifice, I needed to do the best I could to make it as *fine* a gift as possible, not as *big* a gift as possible.

3. I had to accept the fact that I never would be able to have, for example, all of the ice cream I liked. I learned that half a cup contains about 127 calories (some "gourmet" brands contain even more). One pound of fat is accumulated by every 3,500 unneeded calories. Multiply 127 by 365 days and you get 46,355 calories. Divide that by 3,500, and you will come up with 13.2 pounds weight loss a year if you give up a daily serving of ice cream—and don't replace it with something else.

But faced with the need to deny myself a little, I remind myself that many people have much more stringent diet restrictions. There is only one way to treat self pity: kick it out.

4. Other effective, weight control eating guidelines are the following:

Don't skip breakfast. Eating in the morning normalizes sugar levels giving you the energy and attentiveness you need during the day. The ideal plan is to consume 25 percent of your calories at breakfast, 50 percent at noon and 25 percent at night.

Cut your fat intake 30 percent and make it vegetable, not animal fat. Learn to enjoy whole grains, vegetables, and fruits or foods high in bulk but low in calories. You'll feel more satisfied and, eat slower because the food takes longer to chew.

Broil, bake, and steam. Avoid frying and creaming.

Identify what food tempts you to have just a little more and then just a little more. Such foods are probably high in refined sugar. Try giving up these foods completely.

At the same time, it's wise to choose foods to eat that you really enjoy but are lower in calories, and take time to prepare tasty meals. Provide variety. Serve your meals attractively and learn to enjoy mealtime.

There are hazards to avoid when eating out too. Choose restaurants carefully. Those offering Oriental and Middle Eastern foods are best. Decide before you go what you will order. Don't hesitate to ask for lemon on the salad or toast without butter. The customer pays the bill and if you don't ask for the service you need, you'll be paying in other ways.

If you must snack, sit down while eating and don't do anything but eat. Snack breaks should be planned. Snack foods should be healthy and nutritious such as carrots, celery, fresh fruit, or fruit and skim milk shakes.

If you're going to a potluck which most likely will offer only fattening casseroles, eat before you go and then make yourself and others happy by working in the kitchen or waiting on tables.

Change your thinking as to what constitutes a treat or reward. It doesn't have to be dinner out. Instead it can be tickets to a concert, a trip to the mountains, lake or beach, a new garment or book or record, or an appointment to have one's hair styled.

*Discipline* is so important. Accept the fact that for many of us the only solution for keeping our weight under control is hard work. As the writer to Hebrews noted, no discipline is pleasant at first. Some resistance must be overcome. But as one persists, after a while there comes the discovery that a disciplined life actually is enjoyable.

An aid to this discipline has been found in keeping a written list of every morsel that we plop into our mouths. Reporting our progress to others also can help.

Millions of Americans in midlife have discovered the joy of exercise. Exercise is a necessary part of a weight loss program and generally makes us feel fit. Probably the most beneficial, and the easiest to maintain, is swimming, jogging, bicycling or walking briskly for 30 continuous minutes at least three times a week. Paul Dudley White, the eminent heart specialist, has commented: "A five minute walk will do more good to an unhappy, healthy adult than all the psychology and medicine in the world." For added benefit use stairs instead of elevators, legs instead of cars, human energy instead of electrical when possible. If you must watch television, do calistenics while watching. (This might cure excessive watching too!)

## Cancer

Another disease feared almost as much as heart disease is cancer. Nearly one-third of the 350,000 Americans who die each year of cancer could be cured if the disease were diagnosed and treated in early stages. We need to be on the alert constantly for cancer's warning signals:

- A change in bowel or bladder habit
- A sore that does not heal
- Unusual bleeding or discharge
- Thickening or lump in the breast or elsewhere
- Indigestion or difficulty in swallowing
- Obvious change in a wart or mole
- A nagging cough or hoarseness
- Unintentional loss of weight

If you notice any one of these, report it to your doctor at once. A pap smear (test) should be routine for women. Both men and women should ask for a proctoscopy when they have a yearly physical exam to check for cancer of the colon.

## Arthritis

Sooner or later, if we live long enough, nearly all of us are going to be troubled with arthritis. According to the Arthritis Foundation "the patient with the beginning of arthritis who finds the right doctor early before irreversible damage to joints has taken place can be expected to be saved from the serious effects of the disease."

Treatment now generally consists of (1) medications to alleviate symptoms and pain; (2) exercise, posture correction, and physical therapy to prevent or postpone disablement; (3) surgery to rebuild, replace or prevent damaged joints.

*Alcoholism*

An affliction which cripples to an even greater degree than arthritis, because it attacks the spirit and soul, is alcoholism. Alcoholism becomes a special concern for parents not only because of what it does personally, but also because parental use of alcohol can lead children into a trap equally as harmful as drug addiction. Values are learned as children see them modeled every day in every way. Do we have a double standard with regards to drinking—one for ourselves and one for our children?

Statistics have long told us alcoholism is a problem for many in the middle years. Alcoholism reaches a steep 50 percent in the 40-60 age group over the number of alcoholics in their 30s. One of the reasons for this is that it usually takes from 15 to 20 years for a social drinker to become an alcoholic. The earlier one starts to drink, however, the less time it takes to become addicted. Middle-aged alcoholics are found, not only on skid row, but in industry and businesses, among professionals such as doctors, dentists, teachers, and lawyers—even in the minister's study. Ninety-five percent of the alcoholics of our nation live and move—and drive!—in the main stream of society. In any random group at a large public gathering, 5 to 10 percent will be alcoholics, or, in other words, every tenth person you see. Only mental illness and cardiovascular disease are more prevalent among Americans. The danger of alcoholism is becoming greater because social drinking is so acceptable in our society.

Marvin A. Block, former chairman of the AMA Committee on Alcoholism, warns:

> The bald fact is that any drinker, whoever he or she is, runs the risk of becoming an alcoholic, and many people in all walks of life are running the risk and losing. This doesn't mean that this consequence is inevitable in the case of every drinker, but the possibility is always there. This is the first thing that must be recognized by anyone who drinks. To complicate matters, one of the first effects of alcohol is the modifying of judgment. This makes of drinkers themselves poor judges of whether or not they are drinking ex-

cessively. They, as a matter of fact, will usually be the last persons of their families to recognize their changing manner of drinking.

Dr. Block used a questionnaire with his patients to help uncover hidden causes of beginning alcoholism. He graciously granted me permission to reprint those questions here.

1. Is the desire for a drink of frequent occurrence, with the emphasis on the *desire?*

2. Is there need for a drink at certain times of the day with emphasis here on *need?*

3. Is there anticipation of drinking in the evening, as the day wears on?

4. Is alcohol used to help sleep?

5. Does frequent drinking go beyond socializing?

6. Is there a desire to get *high* and thereafter to maintain that plateau through more drinking?

7. Is there disappointment when drinks are not served at a restaurant or a private party?

8. Is there criticism of one's drinking by someone who cares?

9. Is there resort to a drink more when there is discomfort of any kind, as a means of relief from tension, or from physical or psychological malaise?

10. Is care always taken to have a supply of alcohol on hand *just in case* or is there more than slight preoccupation with the consideration?

Dr. Block emphasizes that all who drink should constantly review and evaluate their drinking patterns. If change and discipline are needed, change must be made.

Jackson A. Smith of the Stritch School of Medicine (Loyola University) in Chicago, describes the "social alcoholic" as one who may have a routine martini at lunch, a couple more drinks before boarding the commuter train and again before dinner. There may be wine with dinner, but the drinking ceases with the meal. After dinner the person will sleep soundly in a chair, then awaken to go to bed.

Because the alcoholic usually is unwilling or unable to

detect alcoholism personally, others need to be on the alert. Warning signs at work are lower productivity, an increase in job errors or accidents, a more spasmodic work pace, excessive absenteeism or tardiness, unexplained temporary absences from the work place and leaving work early, frequent Monday absences, irritability and fatigue, and an overall worsening of relationships with others.

The biggest difficulty is motivating the alcoholic person sufficiently to seek professional help. If their employer is sympathetic, the family can work through them. Employers have the power, through threat of firing or demotion, to intervene. Neither logic nor tears will move a person as much as fear of losing their job.

Rehabilitation centers to help the alcoholic and the family can be found in or near every city. I spent a few days visiting Hazelden in Center City, Minnesota. Hazelden combines a peaceful, rural setting with a homelike atmosphere. Skilled and compassionate professional staff give unstintingly of themselves, and because of their sacrificial service, the fees at Hazelden are within reach of almost all. In addition, Hazelden can be justly proud of its record of 65 percent rehabilitation.

There are many other such centers that stand ready to help the alcoholic. Consult the yellow pages of your phone directory, or ask your doctor or pastor.

*Drug Addiction*

Closely related to alcoholism is drug addiction, the creeping menace among middle aged suburbanites. A young man I know is an apprentice carpet layer in apartment units. "We have to work fast," he explained. "One of our men is middle aged, so to maintain the fast pace he keeps dropping pills down his throat. Really," the young man shook his head, "is that the way life has to be?"

Yet the practice has become so prevalent that Dr. Lawrence Smith, a general practitioner from the Los Angeles area, has wondered if the suburban black-market trade in "pep" pills may become as lucrative in sales to those in midlife as it has been to youth. Women use them to elevate moods, to fight loneliness, and withstand the daily grind. Valium, a powerful tranquilizer, is the fourth most frequently prescribed drug in the United States. In addition to Valium, several minor tranquilizers that have recently become available compete for popularity. The use of psychotherapeutic drugs, into which classification many tranquilizers fall, has declined somewhat in the past few years, however, probably due to fear of addiction. The use of anti-depressants has increased, but Americans are taking fewer sedatives and barbiturates, according to Carlene Baum, the principal author of a Federal Food and Drug Administration report released in 1983. At least some of these drugs are classified as addictive, and constant users of them can be considered belonging to the drug culture. Middle-aged people need as much help fighting addiction to drugs as young people.

*For Women: Menopause*

Surprisingly, many are ignorant of the most basic facts about menopause. Menopause means simply the final end of monthly menstruation, the end of a woman's child-bearing period. And that is about all it means. A woman remains a woman.

How does a woman know she is approaching menopause? One indication is when a woman's menstrual periods become irregular or the amount of flow decreases. Physiological side effects are not uncommon.

Some of the unpleasant symptoms associated with hormone fluctuation are depression, sleeplessness, a racing or jerking of the heart, dizziness, frequent and difficult-to-control urination, vaginal dryness or itching, headache, numbness or tingling in fingers and toes, vague aches and pains, and an increase or decrease in sexual desire. Hot flashes perhaps are the most uncomfortable symptom.

Doctors estimate only 10 percent suffer acute discomfort and another 20 percent have moderate symptoms. For most women no drugs are needed, but an understanding of the changes taking place is essential. For those who are acutely uncomfortable, doctors can offer help through medications. Sometimes treatment not only relieves the distressing symptoms but also brings a measure of well-being and good health that a woman may not have known for years. If married, most helpful is the loving, understanding support of a husband who is sensitive and patient, and who leads the children into a kind, caring role toward their mother.

## For Men: the Midlife Crisis

Is there male menopause? Yes, some declare. Nonsense, protest others. How could there be? Perhaps it's a matter of semantics. We might call it the *climacterium* which the dictionary defines as "the bodily and psychic involutional changes accompanying the transition from middle age to old age." Some suggest that it is socio-cultural, that Navajo men, for example, never experience it because they step into a new hierarchy at 45. They become leaders and give orders and advice, but do not have to perform. Many, if not most American men, *do* experience some form of midlife change.

Is it psychological or does a hormonal factor enter in? Daniel J. Levinson, a Yale scientist and psychologist, engaged n an intensive four year study of the midlife crisis of 40 men with five other team members, and defined the different developmental stages of an adult male this way:

(1) Early twenties: "getting into an adult world." The young man is living independently of his parents, but still has not settled what he will do with his life. Friendship with an older experienced man who encourages, helps and influences him is common in this era.

(2) Early thirties: "settling down." Establishing a home is prominent.

(3) From mid-thirties to mid-forties: "becoming one's own man." The man now might chafe under authority and the restraints others place on him. This is the time in life when a man wants most to know he has succeeded.

(4) Mid-forties to fifty: "midlife crisis." The time of questioning and re-evaluation, struggling to accept the disparity be-

tween his dreams and what actually has been accomplished, and asking if it is all worth it.

Symptoms of midlife crisis have been described as nervousness, decrease of sexual potential, depressions, decreased memory and concentration, fatigue, disturbed sleep, irritability, loss of interest and self-confidence, indecisiveness, numbness and tingling, fear of impending danger, excitability and sometimes though rather infrequently, headaches, vertigo, constipation, itching, sweating, and even tears.

If married, a loving, loyal wife who is alert to what is happening to her husband, who understands and who will quietly support and care, can do more than anyone else. "This too will pass." And if the man is aware of what is happening to him, he may be assured of emerging stronger and more purposeful than ever.

*Depression*

Depression weighs heavily on the lives of millions. In this chapter we cannot begin to discuss it adequately, but it is so common we cannot ignore it entirely.

Depression varies in intensity from just being "in the dumps" to agony because those afflicted feel they are so completely different from everybody else. No one knows why, but most depressions go away within weeks or months, the average being 18 months.

One aspect of depression that is not often understood is the rhythm of *highs* and *lows*, or the balance that must take place between excitement and depression. Every high must be followed by a period of depression, which often corresponds in degree of intensity and length of duration with the preceding high. A fact which is even less understood is that not only emotional highs but even accidents involving physical injury and pain can cause an initial excitement followed by depression later on. Knowing this we can better understand those experiences in which persons who have been injured or bereaved are at first in such an exalted state that they seem oblivious to pain. But just as surely, depression will follow. Depression is nature's way of getting us to cut back and slow down so our motor will not burn out.

When we understand that this type of depression is God's gift to keep us in balance, we won't have to go looking for or chasing the devil every time we get down in the dumps. He hasn't brought it on. A normal, chemical reaction in our body has triggered it into being for our own good, to protect and save us. It is true that evil lurks around when we are depressed, because we are more vulnerable then. But we don't need to blame every depression on such direct temptation. Nor do we have to wonder if depression is the result of some sin we have committed. The depression can be received as God's gracious gift to us, a warning signal to slow down. We need to receive it as such, with gratitude, take the cue and get needed rest or turn to some completely different activity which will relieve and refresh us.

When, however, depression persists month after month, for no specific reason (it is natural to feel depressed after one is bereaved or weak after a long illness), it is a good idea to have a talk with your doctor. This is especially true if you begin to feel everybody "has it in for you" and that your situation is absolutely hopeless. Or, you may feel yourself becoming more and more tired every week, full of mysterious aches and pains, tension-induced headaches, nausea, insomnia, or diarrhea for which your doctor has assured you there is no physical cause. Don't give up your search for well-being. Ask your doctor to refer you to someone who can help. Other warning signs that your depression is serious are sudden changes in mood or behavior, noticeable to family, friends or co-workers. Poor performance at work also can alert others to your need for help.

Serious mental illness can be treated in private practice through regular therapy or group sessions, at state, VA and private mental hospitals, at mental health clinics and at general hospitals. Your pastor can help you locate an appropriate agency.

**A Few Simple Rules**
To further help maintain overall health in the middle

years, here are a few simple rules to follow.

1. *If you are worried about something, check it out.* Examination, if nothing else, can alleviate fear, even when the examination uncovers a disorder. When a situation is thoroughly understood and there is something we can do about it, it is not as threatening. A positive outlook on life contributes to robust health, so try to get rid of or at least manage your fears.

2. *Don't overlook the importance of adequate rest to avoid constant fatigue.* With general fatigue comes loss of zest for life. Many people find that as they move along through life they sleep less although in fact they may need more rest, more time to recuperate. If they are able to snatch short periods of rest throughout the day they will find this immensely refreshing. It is well known that Thomas Edison claimed he slept only four hours every night, but he cat-napped frequently.

By our middle years we have become so accustomed to the accelerated pace of life that we find it hard to admit we need to change to a slower pace. But if you feel tired, don't fight the feeling. There's nothing sinful about a little "sanctified sloth." Incidentally, I've discovered that a fifteen or twenty minute rest is an excellent substitute for food, especially in midafternoon. And don't forget the importance of short vacations and days away from it all to recharge the body's batteries.

3. *Give attention to good grooming.* How we look affects how we feel. Watch your posture. Make a conscious effort to straighten up. And remember, as John Wesley said, "cleanliness is next to godliness."

4. *If you become ill, allow more time for recovery than you did previously.* The older one becomes, the longer it takes the body to recover.

5. *Don't resent and fight against medical or health restrictions.*

6. *Have a thorough physical exam yearly.* The old adage is still true: "Better safe than sorry."

7. *Don't count on miracles.* People *are* healed through prayer and the work of the Holy Spirit, but this does not mean you should avoid exploring and using every medical solution to your problem.

## We Are Spiritual Beings

While we acknowledge that we contract diseases that cause illness and that natural deterioration takes place with age, we must note that, generally speaking, physicians agree that only about 10 percent of those who come to their offices have a problem which can be treated solely through medicine. Surely this underscores again that we are, first and foremost, spiritual creatures.

Martin Marty has observed: "We want to be whole, to be fully healthy. God can reach us to make us whole only if we begin as forgiven sinners . . . God has to remake us, as it were. He does this when we repent."

But even Christians who know they are forgiven struggle with spiritual problems which, in turn, affect their physical well-being. There is an undeniable link between illness and loneliness, fear, stress, boredom, hopelessness, insecurity, hostility and lack of purpose. If in the autumn of our lives we can pinpoint our weak points and then resolutely and intentionally resolve to work with God at correcting them, we should be able to look forward to robust health during the senior years—barring physical causes for illness that may develop.

Roy W. Menninger in an article "Emotional Maturity" published in the *Physician's Panorama*, outlined seven criteria of emotional maturity. These are summarized below. You might want to use these criteria as yardsticks to evaluate your personal mental health which, in turn, affects your physical health.

1. I am able to deal constructively with reality. I expect to experience some frustrations to accomplish my goals. I can accept these frustrations and learn from them. I do not run from them nor do I become hostile or fight inappropriately (for example by becoming ill).

2. I can adapt to change. I am learning new ways to cope with problems. I am open to new ideas.

3. I am relatively free from symptoms such as unreasonableness, illogical thinking, irrational behavior. I do not suffer from headaches, stomach pains or other physical discomfort for

which my doctor can find no physical cause.

4. I find more satisfaction and joy in giving than receiving. This does not mean I do not know how to receive. My life contains both elements. I make time for vacations, for worship and prayer and for fun. But I also have a purpose for living and challenges so big I have to keep growing.

5. I am learning how to relate to other people, how to accept and profit from criticism, how to lose with grace, and how to win knowing to whom to give thanks.

6. I am learning how to handle anger in a constructive way through activities of work, recreation and creation. I am learning how to deal with feelings of inferiority or guilt which have no justifiable basis.

7. I care about and for, not only my family, but also for people in my community, church, nation and even for those I have never seen who live in distant lands.

**Biblical Resources**

Here are some questions and scripture references dealing with various aspects of health.

1. The apostle Paul knew how to turn obstacles into opportunities. Read Acts 16. What obstacles did he encounter? In what ways did he allow these obstacles to become opportunities and for what purpose?

2. How did Mary, the mother of Jesus, have to adapt to change? See Luke 1:26-38; Matthew 1:18:19; Luke 2:1-7; Matthew 2:13-15; Luke 2:41-51; Luke 4:16, 18, 19; Matthew 14:1-12 (remember Mary's relationship to John the Baptist and the fact that John and Jesus had been born so close together). See also Matthew 12:46-49; John 19:25-27; Acts 1:12 and 2:1-12. According to tradition the disciple John in later years took Mary and fled to Ephesus where she lived until her death.

3. What evidences of illogical thinking, unreasonableness and irrational behavior do we see in King Saul's life? See 1 Samuel 15:17-23; 1 Samuel 18:6-11, 29; 19:1, 11; 24:1-7; 26:2; 28:7-25; 31:1-6. What sins do you think were at the root of Saul's behavior?

4. What was the apostle Paul's passion for living? See Philippians 1:19-26; 2:16-17; 3:8-14; Acts 20:24. How had Paul also been a recipient? See Philippians 1:5; 2:25; 4:10, 14-16, 18; and Acts 22:3-16. What did Paul say about winning and losing? See Philippians 4:11-13; 2 Corinthians 11:21-12:10.

5. How did Moses have to learn how to handle anger? Compare Exodus 2:11-12 and Exodus 3:1-12. Note that Moses revealed his feelings of inferiority: Exodus 3:11; 4:1; 4:10; 6:12; 6:30. How did God try to meet his needs? See Exodus 4:11, 12; 6:2-8. When Moses would not believe what God had told him, what further provision did God make? See Exodus 7:1. How did this lead to trouble later? See Exodus 32:1-14. What can we learn from the example of Moses?

6. Once we have confessed our sinfulness to God and acknowledged our need of repentance, is it wrong to continue to feel guilty because of our sin? See Jeremiah 31:34b; Isaiah 43:25; Hebrews 10:17; and 1 John 1:9.

7. What evidences of caring do we see in the early Christian church? See Acts 2:45; Acts 6:1; 9:39; and 2 Corinthians 8:1-5.

### Additional Resources

About 1,000 consumer-oriented books on health are published annually. In addition there is a massive body of pamphlet and booklet literature from community health organizations such as the American Cancer Society and the Arthritis Foundation. Approximately 100 such organizations produce health-related pamphlets for the public. Both pharmaceutical and insurance companies also generate and distribute pamphlets. Federal agencies, particularly the National Cancer Institute and the National Heart, Lung and Blood Institute have invested sizeable sums in the production of consumer-oriented pamphlets and booklets. Audio-visuals also are available.

Many of these resources are listed in *The Consumer Health Information Source Book* by Alan M. Rees and Blanche A. Young (R.R. Bowker Company, 1180 Avenue of the Americas, New York, NY 10036). The book probably is available in most public libraries.

Listed here is only one resource for each category.

Alcoholism: *Hazelden 1980 Educational Services Catalog.* Center City, MN. Hazelden Foundation, 1980. 74 pp.

Arthritis: *Patient Education Resources on Arthritic Conditions: Booklets and Brochures.* Bethesda, MD: Arthritis Information Clearinghouse, October 1979, 37 pp.

Cancer: *Coping With Cancer: Annotated Bibliography of Public, Patient, and Professional Information and Education Materials.* National Cancer Institute, Bethesda, MD: Cancer Information Clearinghouse, 1980. Pubn. No. (NIH) 80-2129, 113 pp.

Diabetes: *The DAC Index of Diabetes Education Materials.* Cleveland Heights, OH: Diabetes Association of Greater Cleveland, 1973, 186 pp. $10. Updated 1977 with looseleaf inserts.

Nutrition: *Nutrition Information Resources for the Whole Family.* Berkelely, CA: National Nutrition Education Clearinghouse, April 1979. 11 pp.

Drug Abuse: *Publications Listing of the National Clearinghouse for Drug Abuse Information.* Rockville, MD: National Clearinghouse for Drug Abuse Information, June 1979.

Heart Disease and Hypertension: *Catalog of Information and Education Materials.* Bethesda, MD: National Heart, Lung and Blood Institute, April, 1978. DHEW Pubn. No. (NIH) 78-926. 35 pp.

Mental Health: *Publications of the National Institute of Mental Health.* Rockville, MD: National Clearinghouse for Mental Health Information, June 1979, 4 pp.

Women's Health: Cowan, Beliat. *Women's Health Care: Resources, Writings, Bibliographies.* Washington, D.C.: National Women's Health Network, 1978. 57 pp. $4.

Other helpful books include

*There's A Lot More To Health Than Not Being Sick*, by Bruce Larson, published by Word Books.

*Why Waste Your Illness? Let God Use It For Growth*, by Mildred Tengbom, published by Augsburg Publishing House.

*The Power of Positive Thinking* by Norman Vincent Peale, published by Prentice Hall.

*Spiritual Well-Being,* by David O. Moberg. Available from the U.S. Superintendent of Documents, Washington, D.C.

*Health/Medicine and the Faith Traditions,* ed. Martin E. Marty and Kenneth L. Vaux, published by Fortress Press.

**3**

# Early Frost: Disabilities

> *We have only limited control over what hap-*
> *pens to us. We are always standing in a rain*
> *of happenings, some of which falls on us as*
> *blessings, others pelt us with tragic force. The*
> *answer to our human situation cannot be*
> *found in what befalls us, but in the responses*
> *we give to what is happening to us.*
> —Reuel Howe

At times no matter how hard we try, wholeness, well-being and robust health evade us, and we suffer. Statistics tell us only about three percent of those in the middle years are disabled by chronic disease. Only one out of seven men and one of every eight women are limited to some degree. But after sixty-five, even though only fifteen percent are disabled, fifty percent have to live with limitations of varying degrees. Knowing what lies ahead we realize that the critical age is *not* old age, but the middle years. The habits we form and the attitudes we cultivate, the interests we develop, the relationships we build, and the inner spiritual life and resources we develop during our middle years will affect our aging years when we undoubtedly shall face some problems that won't go away. September mornings are the time to prepare.

## Dorothy and Con Trued's Story
Dorothy Trued has known four arthritic, pain-filled

decades. In addition, during the last eight years she has suffered a broken shoulder and multiple bruises in an auto accident, and in her battle with cancer has undergone a hysterectomy, mastectomy, and colostomy, as well as having implants for cataracts. In a wheelchair, she is completely dependent on her husband, Con, for everything.

"Each stage of attrition has been a battlefield of the spirit as well as the body," Dorothy confesses. "I am grateful though for a body that has tolerated strong medicine over a long period of time. I am thankful too that I always have been an optimist. Life is no joke to me, but I feel its pleasing and joyful sides find too little expression among many. So mine is almost a compulsion to brighten somber faces."

"I am grateful too," she continues, "that my husband, Con, has been the kind of helper he is and able to care for me. I call him my conduit, because whatever I need, Con can do it. Together we have fought against a relentless enemy, planning strategy and sharing our defenses. And our congregation! No persons could have had finer Christian friends to support and encourage."

Con himself has had quintuple by-pass surgery and also has suffered from an aneurism. "But I'm back to playing golf," he said triumphantly.

Admittedly, he has to sandwich in his golf playing, because just the process of getting up and going to bed for the two of them consumes half a day. Yet this does not prevent them from participating in other activities, including travel. When I talked to them recently they had traveled halfway across the country to visit a daughter. "Our motto is, there's no point in staying home to die," Con said.

Understandably, in the privacy of their home, Dorothy occasionally has given way to depression. The frustration of decreasing capability sometimes has driven her into brief sessions of rage and bitterness. "I need more faith and patience to cope with such moods," Dorothy confesses. "I have no question about God's presence and care, although I have wondered about his involvement in my physical illness. Prayer is essential to my life although I have tried no unique ways of prayer. I am open to God's healing grace. I would never be critical of those who seek health through faith healing, and I am grateful when friends receive benefits. But for me to make special spiritual efforts to 'persuade God' to heal me is not consistent with my belief in an all-knowing, caring God who knows my needs before I ask him. At some point, it seems to me, I must accept illness and death as something unconquerable, besides being incomprehensible. So I do not feel that if I am not healed, I am either lacking in faith or weak in some spiritual technique. I accept instead God's answer to Paul: 'My grace is sufficient for you.'"

"Hope is one of the consolations of an arthritic," Dorothy adds. "It is a powerful sustainer of life. Few people, I feel, know that better than I do."

"We look at life with God," Con states. "We are fully assured he is in charge. We don't believe he has *sent* illness. Rather life extends different things to each of us, and this is what is our lot. We believe our Lord is a loving Lord, and we seek to greet each morning with the declaration, 'God is good.' He has enabled us to survive."

He paused, then said, "And when we are tempted to think and act otherwise, we simply consider the alternatives. Should we, as was suggested to Job, 'curse God and die'? We know we don't want any of the alternatives. I suppose," he paused, "it may sound a bit strange, but really, we're still enjoying life. We have two wonderful daughters. They and their families and our friends mean a great deal to us."

## Reinhold Niebuhr's Comments on His Illness

Reinhold Niebuhr, the well-known professor of Applied Christianity at Union Theological Seminary in New York City, wrote of his experience following a stroke that lamed his left side. Initially, said Niebuhr, he was plunged into depression, in fact, three times he experienced deep depression. His neurologist assured him this was quite normal. Friendly psychiatrists told him the chief problem he faced was to reconcile himself to what had happened. Niebuhr found this difficult. He confessed his early response was not reassuring for his ego. "My experience is that constant illness tends to preoccupation with one's ills," he wrote. "The tyranny of invalids is a well-known phenomenon."

He was embarrassed, however, that he could not follow what he had preached. His embarrassment was accentuated because many reminded him of a prayer he had written several years earlier. The prayer was: "God, give us grace to accept with serenity the things that cannot be changed, courage to change the things that should be changed, and the wisdom to distinguish the one from the other."

However, when he finally was able to accept his disability, he experienced no more depression even later when he suffered further impairment. Niebuhr also found himself looking at his former hectically busy life with different eyes. He was forced to reflect and re-evaluate. His wife often had protested when he had dashed off to speak at yet another conference. His typical answer had been that it was important that he go. Now, he wrote, he began to wonder if the reason he continued accepting invitation after invitation was not more that being invited flattered his vanity, and he wanted the invitations to continue to come.

Forced to sit in the pew instead of standing in the pulpit, he gained a new appreciation of and felt the need of a worship service in which he could participate actively, and which would catch him up into the mystery and transcendence of God. He discovered, that for him, the pulpit no longer commanded the central place.

Niebuhr noted too that those who are crippled by heart disease, or any other serious malady, cannot avoid thinking about death. He said that his closest friend, who was in the same situation as he, often talked with him about death. "We declared that we believed in both the immortality and the mortality of the person," Niebuhr wrote.

We die as do all creatures. But it is precisely our anxious foreboding of our death that gives us a clue to the dimension of our deathlessness . . . Our New Testament is confident of "the resurrection of the body," thus emphasizing the integral unity of the person in body and soul . . . I am personally content to leave the problem of deathlessness in the frame of mystery, and to console myself with the fact that the mystery of human selfhood is only a degree beneath the mystery of God.

Niebuhr spoke also of his amazement at the number of people who went out of their way to help and showed "an almost charismatic gift of love." He paid high tribute to his wife and credited her with being his chief source of spiritual strength. "We had been happily married for two decades," he explained, "but I had never measured the depth and breadth of her devotion until I was stricken. The physical ills that consigned me to the 'sidelines' were productive in furnishing me with insights about human nature that had never occurred to me before."

### John's Story

Many who are disabled early struggle with financial problems. Although John had undergone post status aorta coronary bypass surgery, still he was incapacitated by coronary atherosclerosis which caused innumerable small strokes. John referred to their financial problems.

"One very heavy frustration which continued for over a year," he shared, "was the mountain of forms and paperwork required for pensions, insurance policy and Social Security. The stress caused by this was more than I could handle in my weakened condition. My wife had to take over.

"No one had even hinted of the frustrations that would accompany applying for Social Security disability. In the end, we had to hire a lawyer. Even then our first and second requests were turned down in spite of all the cardiologist reports. I then was ordered to appear at a court hearing. At that point we decided to forget the whole thing. Small strokes were hitting me frequently, and I did not feel up to a court appearance. However, the judge finally decided to hold the hearing in our home, and, as a result, I was granted disability. The Social Security check, together with my pension, my wife's salary, and some savings, keeps us going. We have learned that we do not need as great an income as we had thought. Material possessions have become less important to us. We spend less money. God supplies all our needs, though not necessarily all our wants. He has been faithful."

Persons who suffer debilitating illnesses often struggle with feelings of worthlessness. John said the assurance that he was in God's hands brought peace. "I have opportunities to talk with people about Jesus," he said. "My devotional life is rich. I pray for a host of people. My wife and I have developed a tract ministry, and we also give away Bibles and portions of scripture. And I find myself having time to enjoy many things I didn't have time for before.

"At first I needed to spend considerable time resting. I listened to tapes of the Bible and to music. As I gradually became stronger, I started to read, take short walks and do small chores. I have enjoyed visiting different churches. I am able to do some studying, and enjoy this. I also write letters and thoroughly enjoy visiting with our children and grandchildren. How thankful I am for all this!"

John also referred to the bulwark of strength and support his wife has been to him. "She learned to turn over each episode to God," he said. "She gave me to God, placed me and my health in his loving hands. That released her from debilitating worry."

## Lillian's Experience

Sometimes it is the illness or disability of a child that imposes added strain on a family. Lillian recounts this type of situation.

"Todd was our second baby. When I nursed him, I wondered why he seemed slower in responding to my smiles than our daugher. Then one day I set Todd in the baby play table and put a rubber squeak toy on it for him. He made no effort to grab the toy. I squeaked it, and immediately he began to thrash around with his arms, trying to locate the squeak.

"I almost panicked. I ran to the phone and called my husband, Eric. He suggested I make an appointment with our doctor. I didn't know it then, but that appointment was just the first of a series of confusing, conflicting consultations.

"Our family doctor thought Todd's eyes were normal. An eye specialist found the optic nerve atrophied and thought he detected cerebral palsy. Another specialist said, no, it wasn't cerebral palsy. But he thought Todd was both blind and deaf. This neither Eric nor I could believe. Todd responded vigorously to sound. At last we took Todd to the Mayo Clinic. There doctors agreed Todd was blind. There were no further complications, but there also was nothing they could do for him.

"In one way, Eric and I were relieved. We had researched the problem thoroughly. At least we wouldn't be haunted by the guilty feeling that perhaps we hadn't done all we could. "But the joy of having a son was now tinged with sadness. Life never could be as light-hearted or as happy for us again.

"The first six months were hardest. My feelings toward Todd became warmer, gentler, more protective. My love was strong; his blindness never repulsed me. But I found it hard to accept. I would wake up in the middle of the night, Todd's blindness at the forefront of my consciousness. I would cry, 'No! No! No!'

"My biggest problem was that I faced every conceivable situation I could think up without waiting for the situation actually to develop. Would we have to send Todd away to school? How would he take it when he could never play ball? Or drive a car? Would he ever be able to date? Marry? Earn a living?

"One day a woman from an assoication of blind parents invited me to their meeting. I sat and listened to parents making plans for their blind children. They thought the kids could do so many things! I discovered their children were enrolled in regular public schools with a resource program for visually handicapped children. Their calm, positive approach impressed me. I began to see glimmers of hope.

"At the same time I realized I had to face only one day at a time. When I asked myself if I could trust God to see me through the present day, I could answer yes. Then I knew I had cut my problems down to size and I would be able to handle the situation.

"We moved to a new home. A man came to pour a cement slab for the patio. I had Todd outside, and we began to talk about his blindness. This man leaned back on his heels and reminded me of the story of blind Bartimeus and Jesus [Mark 10:46-52], how Jesus had said this had happened for the glory of God. I felt comforted and began to look for ways whereby God would be glorified. I began to give thanks.

"When Todd was five, we enrolled him in a regular public school. Again misgivings and doubts plagued me. Would he be able to cope in a classroom with sighted students? Wouldn't he feel all alone with his Braille books?

"I determined to learn Braille. In class I discovered that not one of my classmates was a parent of a blind child. They simply wanted to help the blind. That overwhelmed me. I had never dreamed other people would be that concerned. I guess people caught in a crisis situation or tragedy feel very alone.

"We soon realized one of the biggest temptations for Todd was to let himself be coddled. Eric kept insisting that self-pity is a luxury none of us can afford. Through the years Todd has been pretty good about this, but sometimes he has expected special allowances from others. We always discourage this.

"Eric has felt that to be of the most help to Todd he has had to put a step between Todd's affliction and himself—that is, he has to remain somewhat objective. I, however, tried to identify with Todd as closely as I could. At the same time, I've discovered that a tenuous boundary divides a vicarious relationship from a smothering, over-solicitious one.

"Did Todd's blindness shake our faith? Yes. Questions came. The only way we could find peace was to bow to God's will, even though we can't understand it now. By faith we accept what has happened.

"In one sense, after tragedy strikes, life will never be the same again. But we can move on to explore ways by which life can become richer than it would have been had this tragedy not come. Because I learned Braille, for example, for years I had a job transcribing books into Braille. It was rewarding for me to think I was doing something for those who couldn't see to read, and it gave me employment as well.

"Todd has unusual insight and perception. Because he cannot be influenced by a person's appearance and mannerisms, he is better able to discover the real person. When he was in his midteens he frequently found himself in the position of counselor to those three or four years older than he.

"A friend offered to teach Todd to play the paino. I brailled out the scores. So rapidly did he progress that we soon had to seek more skilled help. He plays Bach, Beethhoven, and Chopin as well as popular music, and for years has played in a dinner house.

"The patrons know little of the hours of infinite patience spent feeling out and memorizing score by score. Often frustration becomes more than he can bear. Then he pounds the piano thunderously. When he was living at home I had to remind hm that other people lived in our house too, and tantrums are hard on all of us.

"I don't want to give the impression it has been easy. It hasn't. Todd has succeeded only because of his determination. That very determination can make it miserable for parents sometimes. And sometimes he can become so big-headed, it's almost insufferable. Then I have to remind myself of his deep need to be assured he is needed and can perform.

"One summer he and his young blind friends made a trip to Europe. We rejoiced when he graduated from university. He found a job and moved into an apartment. Our crowning joy came when he was married to a lovely girl.

"Todd has blessed our lives richly. Looking back over the years, I see that clearly. Now that I think about it, these years have helped me see many things realized I never dreamed possible."

**For Thought and Reflection**

As you think back over the stories of Dorothy, Con, John, Lillian, and Eric, and as you reflect on the statements made by Niebuhr, try to find the answers to the following questions.

1. What attitudes did they find helpful in coping with their situations?
2. What discoveries did they make about themselves?
3. What discoveries did they make about others?
4. What things became of primary importance?
5. What things faded in importance?
6. What units provided most support for them?
7. What attitudes did they try to make habitual?
8. What actions did they take?
9. How were their lives impoverished?
10. How were their lives enriched?

**4**

# Driving on Rain-Slicked Roads: High Level Tension

> *The world is too much with us, late and soon,*
> *Getting and spending, we lay waste our powers.*
> *Little we see in Nature that is ours,*
> *We have given our hearts away, a sordid boon.*
>
> —William Wordsworth

"The pain in my neck has been getting worse. I even get short jabbing pains down my arms now."

"Here?" asked the school district's doctor, her long, sensitive fingers searching for the trouble spot.

"I think the whiplash I got in a traffic accident three years ago must be causing the trouble."

"Three years ago? Where do you teach, Mrs. Rollins?"

"Hartford Elementary."

The doctor nodded. Hartford Elementary, she knew, was an inner city, multi-racial school with blacks in the majority. As the doctor continued her examination she encouraged her patient to talk.

"It was quite a challenge when they offered me the position as principal last year. I thought hard work and proper teaching would put things right."

"Yes?"

"We made progress too. But then I came back this fall and things were worse than ever." A sigh slipped out. Mrs. Rollins stiffened in her chair. "The thing that's hard to take," she burst out,"is that they're my people." From deep within a sob was wrenched out.

The doctor slid a white-coated arm around the woman's shoulders. "You're sure the pain in your neck is from the whiplash?"

"No," said the woman, throwing back her head, "no, it's from my disappointment in my people."

All of us feel the tightening effect of tension and stress. Those in the middle years feel the pressure in unique ways.

Engineers and physicists were the first ones to use the word *stress*. They used it to refer to the severe forces that might be put on a building or bridge, causing it to collapse, for example, from the weight of ice or the power of a violent wind.

Later the medical world adopted the word to describe the pressures people feel when life becomes more than they can handle comfortably.

Hans Selye, the head of the International Institute of Stress Research at the University of Montreal, has defined stress as the non-specific psychological and physical response of the body to any new demand made upon it. To put it more simply, stress is the wear and tear of living.

Sometimes, however, tension strengthens. When I was in Turkey, visiting the sites of the early churches, I saw an example of this in one place. A slab in the overhanging center part of an arch was held in place, even though it was broken in two, by the pressure of two upright columns on either side of it.

People in all ages have experienced stress. Think about Moses and the Israelites being hotly pursued by Pharaoh's armies and backed up against the Red Sea. Other biblical examples include Nehemiah and his men at work on the wall of Jerusalem in the knowledge that at any moment an army might appear with javelins, spears, and bows aimed at them and swords flashing; or Joseph, sold by his brothers and carried away by strangers into a far country. Then there is Jesus, sur-rounded by crowds, misunderstood, questioned, plotted against, betrayed by someone he loved, misunderstood by his own family and living with the knowledge that one day he would be crucified.

Stress is not only normal, it is inevitable. But it is how we react to what happens to us that determines the effect stressful situations have on us. For example, when you are promoted at work you may feel rewarded, affirmed and challenged. That is a positive reaction. Or, you may be fearful, wondering if you can live up to expectations and get along with new colleagues, and you worry as to whether your family will be sympathetic and supportive when new demands are placed on you. Such an experience is a negative reaction.

The baby boy of friends of mine working in Pakistan became ill suddenly and died. A few days later a Pakistani gentleman came to visit them. "We have a saying for difficult times like this," he said. "We say when unfortunate, tragic things happen to us, we can prove to be either eggs or potatoes. Eggs thrust into hot water get hard. Potatoes get soft."

Stress positively received, according to Hans Selye, may be called *eustress* (*eu* meaning *good* as in *euphoria*). Eustress motivates and spurs to creativity. It leads to adaptation, growth, joy, true security, enhanced strength of character and increased ability to react positively to future stressors. So let's acknowledge that we can't eliminate stress from our lives—nor would we want to! That would mean never enjoying a kiss again! But we do need to learn how to manage and use stress.

### Handling Stress in a Positive Way

If we don't learn how to cope constructively with stress, our health may deteriorate. The Psalmist experienced stress from unconfessed sin.

> When I declared not my sin,
> my body wasted away
> through my groaning all day long.
> For day and night thy hand was

heavy upon me;
my strength was dried up as by
the heat of summer.
(Psalm 32:3-4).

Job had more than his share of stressful situations. He broke out in sores. "I have no appetite for food," he said. "Everything I eat makes me sick." His breath got so bad his wife couldn't stand to be close to him.

"See what anxiety and tension did to me," Alice Wright, retired instructor of journalism from Long Beach City College, said to me, holding out her hands, knobby with arthritic bumps. "The last months as I watched my dear mother fail and die, I watched also the joints of my fingers swell and become distorted." Mrs. Wright moved her fingers slowly as she talked. "After mother died, the swelling was arrested. It spread no farther."

Chronic stress, building up over the years, can lead to rheumatism, ulcers, asthma, headaches, insomnia, sinus attacks, upset stomachs and heart problems. The aggravation of diabetes or the emergence of latent TB have been linked to excessive stress levels also. There is research under way to see if a relationship between stress and cancer can be found.

If you want good health, pay attention to what your stressors are and how you are reacting to them. Some persons, instead of doing this, turn to drugs and alcohol or both. Women seem especially vulnerable. They outnumber men in turning to tranquilizers and barbiturates: 31 million women, compared with 18 million men, use tranquilizers; 16 million women use sedatives compared to 11 million men. And 12 million women take stimulants compared to 5 million men. However, men outnumber women two to one in the use of alcohol.

Reacting unfavorably to stressors also can cause accidents. Twenty-eight percent of male drivers involved in fatal accidents were shown to have had violent quarrels with women in the six-hour period before the accident.

Other stressors that precede accidents include serious conflicts with anyone close, tragic events affecting someone loved, work pressure, financial problems (either actual or feared), demotion or dismissal, job promotions and conflict with a supervisor, employer, or fellow workers.

What is stressful depends, in part, on the individual. Administration is stressful for some while for others it is not. Routine work is stressful for one and yet for another it is not. Specific conditions or facts in a given situation also have a major bearing on what is stressful. The noise of my own lawn mower may not be stressful for me, but it may be for my neighbors. Loud music may not be stressful for my teenager, but it may be for me.

That which is predictable is less stressful. We live only a mile or so from Disneyland in California. During the summer there is an explosive display of fireworks at the park each evening. We are so used to it that we scarcely hear it. Guests in our home, on the other hand, jump nervously and think shooting has broken out in the neighborhood.

Our ability to control a situation also determines how stressful it is. When parents have small children in a public place they experience tension because their children's behavior can be unpredictable. Similarly, parents with adolescent and young adult children often feel under heavy pressure because they feel they are only in limited control.

### Common Causes of Stress

There are numerous causes of stress.

*Frustration* is a common cause. Frustration comes when our progress toward some desirable goal is blocked. The more important our goal, the more intensely the frustration is felt. Also, if blocks are unexpected and unanticipated—if we haven't been aware of how difficult it might be to attain our goal—frustrations are greater. The old adage, "Forewarned is forearmed," remains true.

*Change* can be upsetting. Change in hairstyles and clothing styles can raise tension levels as parents of teenagers understand well. But certainly more serious, changes in family structures, technology, sexual values, morals and knowledge provoke tension as well.

*Fear, and anxiety with regard to the future* raise stress levels also. Newspaper and TV editors know how prevalent fear is. For many of them the first question they ask as they consider whether or not to publish an article or news story is: "Does the item threaten security?" It matters little whether the issue is social security or nuclear weapons. If it does, they consider it worthy of space; it will grab the attention of their readers.

But people fear more than the insecurity of the future. They fear failure, pain, old age, terminal illness, children going astray, unemployment. On and on the list goes, all producing stress and tension.

*People crowding* causes stress. Christmas shopping crowds in stores shorten tempers. In Scandinavia there are curious little rodents called lemmings. Every third or fourth year they hurl themselves into the fjords by the thousands. Earlier observers thought they were looking for their ancestral homes in the Atlantic. Now scientists believe that drowning is not the primary cause of their death. Rather, because their numbers have multiplied so rapidly as to cause crowding, they suffer from metabolic derangements. As their brains are affected they wander around randomly and restlessly until eventually they plunge into the sea.

*Specific experiences of loss, failure, and betrayal* like loss of job, health, or the loss of a loved one through death or divorce impose heavy stress.

*Expectations of loved ones and employers* can create almost unbearable tension. A young man related how his father and mother had separated but had come together again recently. He said his father was dreadfully uptight because he lived with the constant fear of doing something that would displease his wife. He had told his son he didn't know how much longer he could hold out.

That parents can cherish unreasonable expectations of their children too, almost goes without saying.

*Conflict* always heightens tension levels. School teachers frequently have students who complain of stomach pains. Talking with them they discover there is quarreling in the home. The quarreling, in turn, may have been caused because the family members were feeling frustrated in other areas of their lives, and they vent their frustrations on their families.

Sometimes *we are the ones who impose unrealistic goals on ourselves.* "Do not think of yourself more highly than you ought, but rather think of youself with sober judgment in accordance with the measure of faith God has given you," the apostle Paul counsels in Romans 12:3. Attempting to do too many things can overload our stress capacity.

A pastor who was suffering from heart problems went to see his doctor who had known him for many years. After the doctor had completed his examination he peered over his glasses at his friend and said, "What you need is a little humility." The pastor admitted he pondered quite a while before he realized that the doctor was trying to tell him to stop playing God, and acting as though all responsibility for the welfare of his parishioners depended on his care and concern.

When other factors contribute to stress, *little incidents or breakdowns* such as leaky faucets, closet doors that stick and misplaced items can be the final cause for a person's erupting. When pressures on the surface of the earth exceed the ability of the rocks to resist, faults or fractures occur along zones of weakness. Sometimes then the shape of the land is completely altered. Similar things happen to persons when pressure exceeds the ability to bear.

### Warning Signs

Warning signs that stress is becoming intolerable are many and varied. Lack of interest in one's work and personal appearance and a greyness in attitude toward life in general are common. "Month after month I have nothing to live for," Job declared (7:3), and "night after night brings me grief." The Living Bible paraphrases Job 7:1-6 thus:

How mankind must struggle. A man's life is long and hard, like that of a slave. How he longs for the day to end. How he grinds on to the end of the week and his wages. And so to me also have been allotted months of frustration, these long and weary nights. When I go to bed I think, 'Oh, that it were morning,' and then I toss till dawn . . . My life flies by—day after hopeless day.

Extremes also are characteristic of stress: inability to sleep or wanting to sleep all the time; constipation or diarrhea; overeating or loss of appetite. Accelerated heart beat, headaches, dizziness, vague aches and pains, heartburn, indigestion, allergy complaints and skin rashes often indicate inability to cope adequately with stress.

Karl Menninger, who, with his father, brother, son and nephews, founded and developed a psychiatric center in Topeka, Kansas, known now all over the world, states that the most important part of any treatment process is diagnosis. *Gnosis* means *knowledge*, and *dia* means *through and through.* Reading, listening, talking and self-evaluation play an important part as we seek to name specifically what is causing our stress to build up. When we have identified causes we ask, which situations can be changed? How? Which cannot be changed? How can we accept and live with situations that cannot be changed?

### A Few Practical Guidelines

1. *Learn how to deal with frustrations and disappointments.* Avoid them if you can. Avoid irritants that contribute to the problem. Repair faucets that drip and closet doors that don't slide evenly. The same principle applies to more complex situations. Identify the root of the problem or issue. Can we do something about it? If so, do it and do it quickly.

2. *If problems defy solution, then accept the situation instead of fighting it.* In his letter to the Philippian Christians Paul declared: "I have learned in whatever state I am, to be content."

Again and again in the Old and New Testaments we can see how God worked in spite of, and sometimes *through*, disappointments and frustrations to bring about his purpose. Consider, for example, Moses' mother having to hide him in the bulrushes and Pharaoh's daughter finding him. Or, as mentioned earlier, Joseph's being sold by his brothers to the Egyptians. The scriptures are full of examples.

We will almost certainly have to learn to accept some of life's little daily annoyances, too. Suppose it irritates a wife that her husband dumps all the screws, nails, ballpoint pen tops, loose change, and other paraphernalia of his pockets in the drawer with his neatly folded socks until the drawer looks like the aftermath of a Midwestern tornado. Chances are she is not going to change him, so why should she keep on trying and wear both partners out in the process. Accept it. Be glad the junk isn't dumped on the coffee table in the living room. Or in the wife's drawer. After all, it's *his* drawer. And it can always be closed. Who else but the two of them knows what it looks like anyway? This leads to the next point.

3. *Keep disappointments and frustrations in perspective.* I remember once when mother was visiting us, and one of our children broke a cup I had prized. I was beginning to you-know-what when Mother said quietly, "It was only a cup." When I had cooled off a bit, she continued. "A cup can always be replaced. And even if it can't, it is only a cup." In a flash I saw what I was doing to my child by my peevish scolding was infinitely more serious than the broken cup. It was, after all, only a cup, and it had been broken accidentally.

Maintaining perspective is especially important during the time children are adolescents and the husband and wife are feeling pressure on every side, both at home and work. Remember, this time too will pass. The kids will grow up. The house will get quiet. Eventually even days of leisure will come with retirement. In the meantime, take a day at a time and try to enjoy each day.

4. *If you are faced with a problem for which you see no solution, put it on the shelf for a while.*

My sister, who is left-handed, could find no one to teach her to knit. She struggled and tried and finally gave up in despair. One night she dreamed she was knitting. The next morning she got up, picked up her needles and clickety-clack, away she went and has been going strong ever since.

We discredit the power of our subconscious to go to work for us, especially with problem solving. Accept Christ's invitation to cast all your cares on him. In prayer commit to God the snarled problem. Drop it. Let it slip down into your subconscious. Turn your attention elsewhere. In due time the answer will pop up—fresh and right. I've seen this happen many times.

5. *Turn interruptions and interferences into opportunities.* With today's busy pace of life and crowded schedules, interruptions and interferences often string us even tighter. But before we think we are uniquely tested, turn to the Gospel accounts of the life of Jesus and notice all the times he was interrupted. Write *interruption* in the margin every time you find one, and then marvel for Jesus constantly turned interruptions into opportunities.

6. *Learn to pace yourself.* Try to understand how much you can do comfortably in a given length of time. Then don't over-program yourself. Pray and seek God's guidance before you make commitments of service. Many people find it easy to become overextended. Learn to say *no* graciously. If you can suggest someone else who could and joyfully would meet the need, you may do so.

If you already are overloaded, take a critical look at your schedule. Ask what you can phase out and plan to do it gradually. Once you have discovered a comfortable load, *don't add anything to it without eliminating something else from your schedule. Don't keep adding.*

7. *Find someone with whom you can talk out your problems.* Remember, the first step toward finding someone might be your listening to others first.

8. *Substitute cooperation for competition.* In Mark 9 we read about the disciples arguing with each other as to who is going to be greatest in the kingdom. Jesus wisely remained silent and let them carry on. But that night, probably after supper, he quietly asked them, "What were you talking about today on the way?" Embarrassed, they fell silent and looked at each other. Then Jesus pointed out the superiority of cooperation over competition when he declared: "If any one would be first, he must be

last of all and servant of all."

Let's face it, substituting cooperation for competition is difficult for Americans. Our society emphasizes the value of the individual. When we emphasize the individual we encourage competition. When we emphasize the community, we foster cooperation.

Competition sows seeds of distrust, envy, strife, tension, and crooked play. Cooperation yields contentment, appreciation, an easing of burdens, encouragement and affirmation even at times of setbacks.

Even husbands and wives can compete. And so can children in a home.

9. *If possible, don't make too many changes at one time.* This is not to say all change is to be avoided. Change helps us grow, keeps us flexible and challenges us. But avoid too many changes at one time.

10. *Make your vacations a time of complete change from your daily routine.* Experiment with short vacations. A weekend, a day away from home and work is beneficial. Even two, three hours can bring relaxation, refreshment and renewal.

11. *Learn to relax your muscles consciously.* Become aware of where you tighten up. Shoulders? Neck? Jaw? Legs? Mouth?

12. *For Christians, worship and directing thoughts God-ward offers perhaps the most significant solution of all in learning how to cope with tension.*

I asked a friend of mine, Conrad Lund, how his Christian faith helped him handle stress. I knew he lived with a crowded calendar, fractured schedules, and commitment to deadlines. Connie outlined four steps:

(1) *I must admit my need, my failure to manage on my own.* The first signs of approaching defeat begin inside one's body. Blood pressure increases, the heart speeds its pace, muscles tense, and other vital signs signal the onset of an overload. Instead of concentrating on holding all of this in, unseen and unnoticed by even my wife and family, I concentrate on agreeing with God about the verdict life is placing before me. "God," I pray, "I cannot handle this. I need your forgiveness for the

pride that makes me avoid you. I need your grace."

(2) *I set my mind on Christ, who is my life.* I picture him in a similar situation. I see that he remains calm, at peace, content, sure of his Father's care, and of the grace of the eternal spirit, enabling him to offer himself in all things to God without blemish (Hebrews 9:14). I then affirm, "I cannot. But God can."

(3) *I review the experiences I have had of God's grace operative and effectual in my life and also pertinent and powerful promises of scripture that come to mind as applicable to my situation.* Thus aided and encouraged, I affirm, "Since God can, I can. I am his, and with God all things are possible."

(4) *I thank God for any and all situations that come my way.* Contentment then becomes a reality, even in the midst of still present distresses. The primary alteration by which all is made new is a change of view. I say, "My times are in God's hands," (Psalm 31:14), and I then rely on the strength and the kindness of his hands. My life is committed to Jesus Christ. I want him to direct, to enable and to assign my life as it pleases him. That realization helps me to see incidents within accidents, opportunities within importunities, and appointments within disappointments.

Learning how to handle stress creatively could be one of the most important lessons we can learn during our autumn years. To a large extent this will determine how long we live and to what degree we shall be able to fulfill our goals and enjoy life. Learning to live with, use, and overcome tension is worth every effort we can make.

### For Reflection and Sharing

1. Think through a typical day from beginning to end. Write down what in that day was worthwhile and satisfying and which you would not want to give up. Share this with a friend.

2. What was frustrating? Write this down. Is there anything that you can do about your frustration? If so, what?

3. Karl Menninger describes five styles of leisure. Which of the following do you employ?

(a) Creative activity not considered work, such as painting or gardening. Sir Winston Churchill said of painting: "Change in what one is doing is the master key. A person can wear out a particular part of his or her mind by continually using it and tiring it, just as a person can wear out the elbows of a coat. One cannot mend the frayed elbows of a coat by rubbing the sleeves or shoulders, but the tired  parts of the mind can be rested and strengthened by using the other parts of the mind."

(b) Self-restoring contemplation, reading, listening to music, or getting out in nature.

(c) Activity restoration such as playing tennis, baking, cleaning the house, or chopping firewood.

(d) Passive recreation as in loafing and sleeping.

(e) Jokes, humor, plays and comedies.

4. People live life in different ways. Which of the types listed below do you think experience the most tension? Explain. How do their stressors differ? Which of these types do you think will adjust best to aging and retirement? Which probably will have difficulty and why?

(a) The achievers. They are ambitious and goal-oriented and will use people to achieve their goals. They have only limited time for family life.

(b) Those who work for reward, applause, or achievement. They are willing to work hard if they are appreciated.

(c) Those who love to nurture people. They are willing to help others achieve their goals. They care how others feel. They love but also need to be loved.

(d) Creative, independent people. They may be indifferent to people or they may be aware of social needs and have a strong sense of mission.

(e) Detached people. They shy away from responsibility, tension, and risk. They are fearful.

Do we see some of these characteristics in ourselves? Have we moved from one type to another during our lifetime? Can you think of examples from the Bible, or from your present life, to illustrate each type? Talk about this with your spouse or a friend.

# 5

## Fall's Foggy Days As Marriage Sags

*All living relationships are in change, of expansion, and must perpetually be building themselves new forms.*
—Anne Morrow Lindbergh

Lois couldn't believe her ears. Her husband, Roger, was standing by the side of her bed, holding out to her a cup of coffee. She thought she had heard him say, "You'll be served divorce papers today," but how could she have heard that? Married 29 years and then divorce?

"Divorce?" she heard herself screaming. "Why?" And she shot out of bed.

She received no answer. Roger already had pushed his way past 19-year-old Gail standing in the doorway and disappeared.

Later, as Lois was speeding along the freeways on her way to work, she recalled Roger's business failures and the years of paying back debts. Roger had wanted so badly to be rich. She had tried to help him. And now this thanks for her loyalty! Hot tears blurred her vision. She took the wrong freeway turnoff but wasn't aware of it. We didn't ever really quarrel, she thought, except over Gail. Gail was so outspoken. "Dad, I'd rather have fewer things and more stability. And see more of you." Roger always exploded when Gail started talking like that. He'd corner Gail. Then she would defend Gail, and Roger would accuse her of loving Gail more than him. *I'm lost!* she thought, suddenly observing the street signs.

Three days later Roger returned home unexpectedly and stayed for three months. Lois outdid herself trying to please him, cooking his favorite foods, catering to his wishes, avoiding conflict. It was then she discovered that another woman was involved, a widow who sympathized with Roger and supported him in his feelings against Gail. Still Lois hoped things would work out.

A business trip took her out of the city three days. She returned to find Roger's closet and drawers empty. A note said, "I've been a failure as a husband and provider."

It was Friday. Lois went into the bathroom and just stood. All life's happenings flashed before her as though on a TV screen. She reached into the cupboard and took out a bottle of sleeping pills and started to pour them into her palm. Her mind flicked on scenes of Gail with little children around her. She began to weep, and with shaking hands poured the pills back into the bottle.

Lois moved into a smaller apartment and arranged to pay the bills her husband had run up on their credit cards. The middle of June she drove to the small simple cabin they had in the desert. There, alone, in 105 degree heat, she cried, screamed, and yelled. She wrote letters and tore them up. She threw away her wedding ring. At last, exhausted and spent, she returned home.

The next week people at her church found out what had happened. A friend took Lois to prayer therapy classes being conducted in their church for twelve weeks. In a small group of eight Lois was asked, "Why are you here?" She broke down and wept.

The sharing, caring, and praying together was a healing experience. One night Lois knelt by her chair. "God," she sobbed, "I need you so! I want to turn my life over to you. I'm sorry I tried to get along on my own. Will you take me back?"

*Of course, I will,* God seemed to say. *Be patient, my child. Let me put the pieces in place.*

Awed, Lois arose from her knees. She went to bed, and for the first time in many months slept soundly.

In August, the day the divorce was finalized, Lois phoned Roger. He invited her for dinner and she went. Gently she tried to share with him what had happened to her. He listened and even let her pray. They continued to meet periodically and to talk and pray. A year later Roger said, "I'd like to remarry you." Lois wasn't sure.

"Can I come to church with you?" he asked.

Lois hesitated but thinking to herself, "If I refuse him, I haven't really forgiven him," she consented.

It was Communion Sunday. They knelt together, and Lois' eyes overflowed again. Later at the church door the pastor enveloped both her hands in his and said, "God bless your communion." Then he turned to Roger and bear-hugged him while Lois unashamedly wept.

"You can't love two women at one time," Lois said to Roger later.

"I've broken things off with the other one," Roger said gently.

They continued to meet and talk. They both read Eric Fromm's book, *The Art of Loving.* Insight into themselves came. They dated frequently, spent a weekend cleaning and painting their desert cabin, laughing and enjoying each other. They began to understand how play and humor recreate and replenish stores of human strength and self-respect. And always they talked and talked and read the Bible together and haltingly prayed.

In September Lois took a vacation. "I have to get away from you and think," she said to Roger.

Remarrying would involve full forgiveness she realized. With God's help I can forgive, she thought. But there were other problems.

During their months of separation she had changed. She had become a person who dared to stand up for her own convictions. She had thought before that the trouble between them caused by Gail had been only father-daughter trouble. Now she was startled as she realized Gail had been vocalizing what she, Lois, had felt all these years. She too really would have been much happier with a steady job for Roger rather than all the risky business ventures. But in her desire to be a good and sub-missive wife, she hadn't said anything. *Why!* she realized now, *I wasn't telling him how I really felt. We weren't working things out together. I had thought a good relationship meant absence of tension and conflict. I had tried to repress my feelings and thoughts, not understanding that life is made up of alienation, forgiveness and reconciliations. Now it can never be the same again. Something has happened to me. I'm a different Lois, a Lois with convictions who will speak out, a Lois to whom God and the Bible and prayer and tithing are important. Will Roger accept the new Lois?*

*Yes* her heart told her. *Roger likes the new Lois. He's tried to tell you all summer.*

*But what if I am hurt again? I can't stand the thought of being hurt again.*

*You have to take the risk,* a little inner voice said. *Have faith. Remember Peter walking on the water? As long as he kept his eyes on the Lord, he was all right.* Trembling, Lois prayed, "I'll risk it, Lord. Just stay in sight for me."

Two months later in a quiet service in the chapel they were remarried.

Lois and Roger's story contains so many beautiful elements in it that we wish it could be typical of marriages in deep trou-ble. Instead many end in permanent divorces.

Perhaps one reason marriages in trouble end more quickly in divorce these days is because it is easier now to get divorces. Many avoid pain, and rather than endure the pain which comes with working out differences, they think divorce is the easy way out. What they do not realize is that if they do not have the courage and faith to face the realities of the first unhappy situation, chances are they will repeat the same mistakes in the second relationship.

The fact that much of the stigma formerly attached to divorce has also disappeared contributes to more frequent divorces too. And without question, TV and the cinema have made their impact also. Frequent viewing of people with low moral standards, who think nothing of exchanging partners or having affairs, especially when things get tough or unpleasant at home, cannot help but condition the thinking of the viewer, until at last he or she embraces the way of life seen portrayed.

However, many still do consider the marriage vows sacred. And many still adhere to the philosophy expressed by the African proverb: "Two civet cats, when they fight, are not to be separated." Or perhaps you have heard the answer given by a couple celebrating their 50th wedding anniversary. A reporter asked if they had ever fought.

"Of course."

"Did you ever consider divorce?"

The wife was astonished. "Divorce?" she asked. "Never!" Then, with a twinkle in her eye she added, "Murder, yes, but divorce? Never!"

What can we do to enhance already happy marriages and strengthen faltering ones? Surveys have shown that satisfaction in marriage climbs when children enter school but when kids become adolescents it drops sharply, to a lower level than at the time of the marriage. The situation improves slightly during the time of launching, when the oldest child is 19. After that there is a steady climb that reaches a high peak during the empty nest period, and then, understandably, as health deteriorates and other factors enter in, the level drops again gradually. But since marital happiness is the lowest during the middle years, it surely behooves all of us to concentrate on our marriages. Here are ten ways to do so that many have found helpful.

## Ten Ways to Strengthen Your Marriage

1. *Be reasonable and realistic in your expectations of life, marriage, and your mate.*

Before I went to India as a missionary a wise man alerted me: "Your missionary career will fall into three stages. The first is the honeymoon phase when you are completely enamored with the country and people. The second phase begins when you start to perceive shortcomings and failures in the people to whom God has called you. To your dismay you may discover they lie, cheat, steal, talk behind your back, live immoral lives, and think nothing of fooling you about all of this. Your disillusionment may be so great you may actually find yourself hating the people, though you would never dare say so. This is a crucial stage. You may give up and go home. You may become cynical. Or you may accept the people as they are and begin to love with common sense."

Most marriages go through similar stages. New love is starry-eyed and unlimited in its expectations. Many believe finding and marrying the right person will answer all of life's problems and bring the ultimate in happiness. But by midlife we have lived through enough Saturdays and Mondays to know married life and heaven are not synonymous. We understand that life is largely made up of routine tasks, of getting up and going to work, of paying bills and wiping up spilled milk and cleaning the house and mowing the lawn and getting up with the kids at night when they are sick. And it is in this sphere of life we find our joyful way. We are realistic about life and reasonable in our expectations—not cynical or bitter—but reasonable.

We are reasonable and realistic in our expectations of others too. "What do you expect us to be—*perfect?*" one of our children sometimes used to ask me. Unfortunately all too often we demand a great deal—perhaps too much from those we love. We need to be reasonable. We do our loved ones the most grievous wrong when we expect them to satisfy the deepest needs and longings of our hearts. Only God can do this.

Remember in Lois and Roger's story that the relationship began to heal when Lois herself found healing in a new relationship to Christ. Christ met her deepest needs. She leaned on him. Herein lies the most absolute and enduring hope for all married couples in trouble. Efforts to bring about healing in a festering or broken relationship would do well zeroing in first on the individual's personal relationship to God. Wholeness there must come first. As we see ourselves and our failings in God's light, we become more tolerant and sensible about our expectations of others. As C. S. Lewis noted, "The Christian faith is a thing of unspeakable joy, but it does not begin with joy, but rather in despair. And it is no good trying to reach the joy without first going through the despair." We need to learn to know ourselves as we really are—sinners in need of grace and forgiveness, and then we need to know how to appropriate the forgiveness God offers us. Then we can begin to relate to people in the same way God relates to us.

2. *Accept your mate as a person rather than assigning stereotyped characteristics and roles to him or her.*

One thing that has meant much to me in our marriage has been my husband's granting me freedom to be myself. He encourages me to be the distinct, unique human being God meant me to be. He has never forced me into either a stereotyped mold or one of his own choosing. He has respected me, valued the abilities God has given me, and encouraged me in every way to become a whole person.

3. *Husbands and wives need to be good forgivers.* We need to for our own sakes. Even if forgiving doesn't change the one we feel has offended us, still it does change *us.*

I have a friend whose marriage has given much occasion for forgiveness on both sides. Communication still is not the best, but the situation is becoming more tolerable. And my friend is slowly discovering an inner core of peace because she is forgiving. She is learning slowly to thank God for all. I have faith to believe that in the end the forgiving, accepting spirit she is struggling to make her habitual response will win out, and their family will know a degree of happiness they have not known before.

In her case much of the trouble stems from not having learned early in life to resolve conflicts when she encountered them. The admonition in Proverbs to "not let the sun go down on your anger" is wise counsel indeed. Forgiving is best done on a daily basis. Clear the air before you go to bed and surely before you go to sleep. Don't let unconfessed and unforgiven resentments pile up. If you do, you'll soon have a high brick wall to tear down.

My friend also used to think she should openly vent all the

things she was feeling and thinking. Explosions were common. Now she is realizing the value of self-control, of sometimes keeping her mouth shut while she is still angry, of working off her frustrations by vigorous exercise or work, and waiting to discuss matters of disagreement until she has cooled off. And even then she watches what she says and how she says it.

4. *To be happily married requires both time and effort.*

A good experience in a Christian group can be a soaring experience. Sometimes a person asks, "Why can't I achieve this warm, close, melting relationship with my mate?" One explanation is that when we join a small group we commit ourselves to giving a sizeable chunk of time to the group. Perhaps if we gave equally as much time to our mates we would grow in a warm or more intimate relationship with each other.

I asked many middle-aged couples what they considered the single greatest factor in the breakdown of a happy married relationship. The answer given most often was *breakdown of communication.*

What is to blame for lack and breakdown of communication?

"Taking each other for granted, going separate ways, and not bothering to share thoughts and feelings with each other," one said.

"The TV," many insisted.

"It's the dishwasher," one grandmother declared, wagging her finger. "Before we got the dishwasher everybody in the family had to take turns washing, wiping, and putting away. We sometimes complained, but we sure got a lot of visiting done too."

"It's convenience and snack food," another mother complained. "We sit down together for a meal only three times a week at the most."

"It's outside activities," another declared. "The Elks. The Optimists. Church activities. PTA. Boy Scouts. My husband and I write notes to each other."

"Many times it's not intentional," another said. "But going to night school, working at second jobs, or husband and wife both working can contribute to it too."

A man snorted. "If women and kids were content with less, we men wouldn't have to work so hard and our women wouldn't have to work either!"

"I think a question all of us need to ask ourselves periodically in regard to our activities," one of the women said, "is, 'Is what I am doing now good for our marriage?'"

Whatever the hindering factor is, the fact remains that good marriages, like all other things of excellence, take time. What can we do about it?

One happy couple took a weekend away from the family every month or two as long as the children were young enough to be in the home. "How could you afford this?" I asked. "We couldn't afford not to," they answered.

Another wife greets her husband with a cup of tea when he returns from work every afternoon. The two of them spend 15 or 20 minutes together, talking, sharing. The children have grown up knowing this is Mom and Dad's time together.

Sharing work can draw a husband and wife together, or they can develop new and broader avenues of service together or find something else of common interest.

Little customs, common perhaps in the early years of marriage but since forgotten, can be revived: a telephone call in the middle of the day, unexpected flowers or gifts, dressing for dinner, a ticket to a play, a gift.

5. *As you talk, make a conscious effort to understand one another.*

To understand and be understood is one of our basic human needs. "No one can develop freely and find a full life," Paul Tournier, noted Christian doctor from Switzerland states, "without feeling understood by at least one person. Misunderstood, we lose self-confidence, we lose faith in life or even in God. We are blocked and we regress."

To understand what your mate is really like will require a life-time. This is true because we are constantly changing. Some scholars believe our personalities change most between the ages of 25 to 35. If we cease to share with one another what we believe and how we feel about things, we will not know how the other has changed. One of the characters in Lillian Hellman's play, *Toys in the Attic*, says sadly, "Well, people change and forget to tell each other. Too bad—causes so many mistakes."

Understanding requires a lifetime also because we grow in trusting each other more. Sometimes it takes a long, long time before we dare reveal ourselves even to those we love most.

I recall an attractive, well-educated wife of twenty years telling of an experience. She and her husband considered themselves happily married. They frequently spent hours talking and sharing. Then one day a lecturer came to their church, a quiet, perceptive man. The couple, who had known him casually before, invited him home for coffee.

"As the evening progressed and the talk deepened, I sat and listened with awe," the wife said, "as I heard my husband share cherished dreams and hopes and encounters he had had with God about which I had known nothing. It was as though I were listening to a stranger, and with not a little grief I wondered why he had not been able to share this with me before."

To understand another person requires first *wanting* to understand. Actually this is far more difficult than one realizes, especially if years of unhappiness, tension, and a breakdown of communication have preceded. We are all interested primarily in ourselves. To become truly interested in others requires effort. Besides, as we begin to understand another, we might see the need of *our* changing. We do not always welcome this.

If we really want to understand and know the other person, what should be our next step? First, begin to pray for the person. Pray for understanding. Ask God why the person acts and reacts as he or she does. Then be quiet and listen. As you do, you will be amazed how God enables you to see things from the other's perspective.

Next, we need to learn how to listen. Listening means holding your tongue, not responding quickly with glib pieces of advice, and surely not interrupting.

Listening means withholding judgment and criticism. Several weeks may pass before you hear the story that will explain what you have heard today. Be patient.

Listening can be done with the confident faith that you are helping the other by listening.

Listening sometimes means communicating non-verbally—getting a message when no words are spoken. We need to be sensitive to moods, to expressions on faces. We learn to interpret them and become aware of needs.

As we listen, *we* also must begin to share. We must go beyond talking on the periphery and share the "really, really me," not fake it. It is because we haven't done this that we sometimes have become very lonely.

Sharing involves risk. What if the other person does not understand? It is a risk we must take if we are to grow in understanding of each other.

Some couples have found it helpful to pray together. Astonishingly few couples do. They may pray with their families or in other groups, but few pray together alone, just the two of them. I wonder why? Do we fear the exposure and honesty that true prayer requires? Yet if we will but let go of our pride in this respect, we shall find new life together and with God.

I know of one young Christian couple who handle every disagreement by promptly getting down on their knees and praying togther before too many angry words are spewed out.

6. *Understand what is important to your mate. Then show that you care.*

Ask yourself, What can I do to make my husband's face glow with appreciation and pride? What will cause my wife to hug and kiss me spontaneously and joyously?

My husband repeatedly has encouraged my writing. It was he who bought my desk, filing cabinet, and even negotiated for a larger home so I could have my own quiet study for writing. His latest gift was a home computer to use for word processing.

We will find often that what is meaningful to others doesn't cost money, however, but time and expression. One of my fondest memories of childhood was my father at the end of a meal reaching over to pull mother on his knee as he told her how good the meal was. No wonder our meals became more and more delicious.

Norman Vincent Peale speaks appreciatively of the neat house his wife keeps for him. He says he can't work well if there is disorder around. For other husbands it might be as simple a thing as perked coffee instead of instant, entertaining their friends, suits in press, telephone messages promptly relayed, *not* talking to him when he first comes home, cessation of nagging, no overdrawn bank accounts, peace and quiet. And wives of course have plenty of special needs too.

We need, however, to emphasize the importance of thoughtful, wise expressions of love. A woman was critically ill in the hospital for a long time. Her husband knew she wanted new draperies for the living room. He ordered new draperies for her coming-home surprise. They were a completely different type, color and design from what his wife had dreamed about. She didn't like them, but was hesitant to express her feelings. In this case, letting the wife make her own selection would probably have been more meaningful than the element of surprise.

7. *Have a happy sex life and learn how to handle temptation.*

Some behavioral scientists believe we live in a time of over-emphasis on the importance of sex in married life. A number of middle-aged church people, and women especially, have not had a happy experience with sex in marriage and they need help. Why have many only endured sex? Several reasons contribute to this.

Some people simply do not know how to express love in a spontaneous, caring, natural way. Love is an intense, secret, silent emotion for them—whether toward God or people—not to be expressed openly and freely, and rarely playful.

It is not easy to shake loose from these inner, restraining forces, long a part of our emotional make up. We might not even be aware of them, except that we know our response is not what it could be. But God can liberate us as we bring the matter to him. In mysterious ways he is able to reach into the deep recesses of our being where we are helpless to effect change and set us free. Loving sexuality is a work of grace.

Because unfaithfulness in marriage is ever more evident among those in the middle years, we need to consider briefly how to handle temptation. Temptation may come to the person in midlife because the person has not understood the necessity of satisfying the continuing need for adventure. If the need for adventure is not met, frustration and boredom set in. Life becomes blah. It is then that sometimes the need for adventure becomes so strong the person, perhaps unconsciously, seeks to satisfy the need in wrong ways. Having an affair is one of the most common.

Temptation will come also because we are capable of being attracted to many people. There is no such thing as being able to feel love and admiration for only one person, nor is there anything sinful in attraction. Emotions are fickle. You cannot *decide* that you will not be attracted, or that you will not feel love, hate, anger, admiration or fear. These emotions will wash over you, sometimes threatening to innundate you. But you *can* control what these emotions continue to do to you and with you.

Usually a person in the middle years cannot feel strong attraction for someone of the opposite sex without knowing it. There are a very few naive individuals who do not seem to be aware of their response until they are too deeply enmeshed to get out easily. But generally speaking, a middle-aged person is neither a novice lover nor a teenager. We *know* our response. The time to nip temptation is the first moment we become aware of our response. This is difficult to do because the attraction is pleasurable. We want to at least play with the thought, to fantasize, to turn to it when we are bored, when our mate irritates or does not satisfy us, or before we go to sleep. Such pastime, we argue with ourselves, is innocent and harmless. Nobody will know we are doing it. We assure ourselves we have no intention of going beyond the thought.

Now this can be dangerous even for those who are happily

married. For those who are not, it is like placing a pan of gasoline on a lighted stove. Not without cause did Jesus write: "Anyone who looks on a woman to lust after her in his heart has committed adultery with her already in his heart." (Matthew 5:28)

The temptation must be stopped with the pleasurable thought. But outward action should be taken too. Physical distance—and I mean miles—must be put between the two attracted to each other, no matter what the cost. Move the family. Change jobs. No sacrifice is too great. The move must be made. Separation must come about. The two should not be able to see each other. And then attention must be directed towards correcting and improving the original marriage relationship.

Perhaps our insistence that temptation must be recognized has not been strong enough and we have not dealt with it drastically *before* it becomes sin. We have become so indulgent and accepting of divorce that we let temptation walk in the door and think nothing of it till it has us trapped. Even then we are "broad-minded" and "understanding."

Admittedly, there are certain circumstances where divorce is the only solution. But aside from these cases, the marriage vows should be regarded as binding on one for life. Divorce, in any case, is shattering. It wounds and kills. It can stunt and embitter. It adds burdens to life and produces many new problems.

The Christian in his middle years who is bored or unhappy with his marriage should earnestly seek ways of bettering it rather than quickly and easily casting it aside in favor of starting afresh with another union. *If we do not have courage and faith to face our past problems and failures, chances are great we shall repeat the same mistakes in a second relationship.* And today, more than ever, many stand ready to help us.

8. *Recognize that adverse situations sometimes have caused the problems that arise. Stop blaming each other or yourself.*

Sometimes a child or children can become divisive factors in a marriage. If a parent is having problems with a child, he or she may feel out of control. This produces frustration. The frustration may be vented, not only on the child, but on the innocent mate, and the bewildered mate wonders what he or she did wrong now.

Learning more about each other's childhood and early years can help us understand how these too might be causing difficulties in our marriage relationship. Couples need to recognize also that strong forces in our present society are at work to cause marriage relationships to disintegrate. In fact, in many cases the stresses of life have become so complex that couples will need to seek help.

9. *Find substitute extended families who can help and encourage.*

"Many hands make light work," is true in regard to the help, encouragement and support sympathetic, understanding relatives can give us in raising our families. This is true for sunny days and even more so for days of trouble.

But for many of us today hundreds, even thousands, of miles separate us from our relatives. We live as isolated family units. We refer to the small family unit of father-mother-children as the nuclear family, and the larger family which embraces grandparents, aunts, uncles and cousins is called the extended family. An extended family can do much to strengthen the nuclear family. The children do not experience as much peer pressure from other conflicting groups if they are surrounded by cousins who are reared with the same values they are. Like-minded uncles and aunts strengthen and reinforce the parents' stand. There may be less rebellion among the children.

Sometimes another adult family member will be closer in age to the child than the child's own parents and may understand the child better. "You don't understand me!" How often parents hear this! Sometimes parents *do* understand, but the child doesn't realize it. Sometimes parents *don't* understand. Children in school often are being subjected to teachings and values so different from what their parents were that chasms of misunderstanding can develop. If small nuclear families limit themselves to their own inadequate resources, someone in the family is sure to suffer. Within the circle of a large extended family the child has far better chances of finding someone who can understand him or her and then tensions in the family, as a result, will be less also.

Emotional needs are met by the extended family. Grand-parents may be more accepting, tolerant, and patient than parents. They have more time to look at bugs, listen to ques-tions, and take delight in their grandchildren. Aunts and uncles have varied interests. If they are unmarried, they often share their income with their nieces and nephews, taking them on trips and tours the parents cannot afford. During these excur-sions the child's life is enriched by intimate asociation with another family member who is loved, trusted and often ad-mired. And with the child away for a while the husband and wife have a little breathing space in which to enjoy each other.

Many of us, however, are going to have to learn to live as isolated single family units and still survive. One solution is to find a substitute extended family. Our family has found it in God's people.

Some criticize the church saying the many activities separate and pull apart a family. Perhaps over-indulgence in church activities can contribute to this, but it has been our ex-perience as a family that the activities and opportunities for study, worship, service, and fun which our church has offered us have strengthened our family unit.

I always have been grateful when the local church met some of the needs of our children, needs which I would have found dif-ficulty meeting. I have been appreciative of church school teachers who have loved and been tuned in to our children. I have admired and appreciated youth counselors who actually seem to have enjoyed overnighters with our young people, who have taken them to the beach or mountains for a whole day. I have rejoiced over the listening ears and understanding hearts our young people have found in peer friends and young adult friends at church. I have been grateful to pastors who through ser-mons and teaching have upheld the same moral standards we do, and also have helped our children grow in faith and grace. And I continue to cheer every one who loves Jesus and encourages our children to do so. By so doing they strengthen the emphasis my husband and I have sought to give.

My husband and I also have found among God's people

friendship and love different from what we experience in our home. Through sermon and Bible study our sights also are being constantly lifted. We are expected to stretch and grow, so we stretch and grow. We are encouraged when downhearted, supported in trouble, loved, and accepted. Our lives have been immensely enriched. Our marriage has become more meaningful and our family life the deeply happy and rewarding one it is largely because of our close associations with God's people whom we have found usually in the fellowship of the organized church. So while we miss our extended families and suffer some impoverishment because we are not near them, we have found a blessed substitute indeed in God's family.

10. *Set family goals.*

"Love does not consist in gazing at each other but in looking outward together in the same direction," Antoine de Saint-Exupery declared.

The home and family should never become an end in itself, but rather the base from where we serve God. Too much attention paid to family relationships can itself breed trouble. Why is there such a high divorce rate among marriage counselors? Could one reason be that they are always concentrating on marriage problems?

No matter how troubled or happy we are in our home relationships, we do well not to limit our interests to the home. In turning outward and in seeking to help others we, in turn, will find life. We can set family goals and then work together to accomplish these goals.

We have considered ten ways in which to make a good marriage better and strengthen a weak one. Time and money spent in solidifying marriages will, in the end, be the most significant gift that can be given to children. If we are happy together, we shall be better parents. We also shall be teaching them lessons about married life, setting patterns for them to follow.

The relationship between husband and wife is unique. Anne Morrow Lindbergh states: "It is not two turned outward though pulling together. It is rather two complete individuals facing life together."

If midway through our married years we want this to be

our goal, we do well first to stop and thoughtfully and prayer-
fully re-evaluate our married life as it is now. Hopefully the
questions listed below will help you begin to do this.

## For Reflection and Evaluation

Paul Tournier has these comments to make on inter-
personal communication. They are from his book *To Understand Each Other.*

People are always much more sensitive than we
believe them to be. Often men are just as easily hurt as
women, even though they hide it. They are afraid of
being hurt by advice just as much as by criticism. They
resent it every bit as much. A woman for whom everything seems clear-cut, who confidently tells her husband how he must act in order to do the right thing, no
matter what the problem may be—such a woman gives
her husband the impression that she thinks him in-
competent. No husband can put up with this.

In order to really understand, we need to listen,
not to reply. We need to listen long and attentively.
In order to help anybody to open his heart, we have
to give him time, asking only a few questions, as carefully as possible, in order to help him better explain
his experience. Above all we must not give the impression that we know better than he does what he
must do. Otherwise we force him to withdraw. Too
much criticism will also achieve the same result, so
fragile are his inner sensitivities.

There are also husbands who say, "I do not want
to burden my wife with worry; I keep my problems
to myself." These husbands may be sincere in thinking thus, but they are deluding themselves. There are
always deeper reasons for such inner blockage of con-
fidences. In any case it is a sign that the marital sharing has failed. A woman can bear any anxiety when
she feels supported by her husband and meets every
blow head on, along with him. The worst worry for a

woman is perhaps that of feeling that her husband is weighed down with problems which he does not share with her. There are many misunderstood people in this world. But when we look at them close up, we realize that they are always at least partly responsible themselves. If they are not understood, it is because they have not opened up.

1. Do men agree with Tournier's observation in the first paragraph?

2. Do women agree with his insights in the third paragraph?

## For Husband and Wives to Consider

1. How do you show romantic interest in the other person?

2. How often do the two of you sit down and talk about how you feel about certain things that concern you?

3. In what ways are you trying to help each other develop your Christian lives?

4. How are you sharing responsibilities?

5. How often do you tell each other, "I love you"?

6. When did you last compliment your spouse?

7. In what ways do you show courtesy to your spouse?

8. What do each of you consider the best aspects of your life together?

9. What are the weakest parts?

10. From the categories listed below, indicate those in which you think you find most agreement with each other. In which ones do you experience conflict to the degree that you think these areas need some attention?

Realistic expectations.

Matters of finance.

Communication.

Liking and getting along with each other.

Sharing leisure time and interests.

Sexual relationships.

Mutual sharing of responsibilities and decision-making.

Christian faith.

Good relationships with families and in-laws.

Good relationships with children and agreement in disciplining.

Ability to discuss matters about which you disagree.

**Resource Books:**

*To Understand Each Other*, by Paul Tournier (John Knox, 1963).

*The Creative Years*, by Reuel L. Howe (Seabury, 1969).

*Gift From the Sea*, by Anne Morrow Lindbergh (Random House, 1978).

*Love Is a Couple*, by Chuck Gallagher (Doubleday, 1978).

*Love*, by Leo Buscaglia (Fawcett, 1982).

*If I Were Starting Our Family Again*, by John and Betty Drescher (Abingdon, 1979).

And by John Powell, published by Argus Communications:

*Why Am I Afraid to Tell You Who I Am?* (rev. ed., 1969).

*The Secret of Staying in Love* (1974).

*Why Am I Afraid to Love?* (1969).

*Unconditional Love* (1978).

*Fully Human, Fully Alive* (1976).

Many couples have found weekend marriage retreats helpful in strengthening relationships. Several denominations have Marriage Enrichment programs. For information, check with your pastor, or write:

Association of Couples for Marriage Enrichment
P.O. Box 10596
Winston-Salem, NC 27108

The Marriage Encounter movement is also popular, although it uses a more structured setting of interaction between husband and wife. National Marriage Encounter, 955 Lake Dr., St. Paul, MN 55120 is a loose knit ecumenical organization. Worldwide Marriage Encounter, Inter-faith Board, 8695 Hideway Lane, Centerville, OH 45459 has a strongly Catholic identity.

## 6

# School Begins:
# Steps That Lead Away From Home

*Believe me, it's a long apprenticeship learn-
ing to love.*

—Michel Quoist

"Why do you still set a time for me to be in at night? Don't you trust me?" Nineteen-year-old Beth, her dark eyes flashing, stood facing her mother, fingering her keys. Beth's reaction, typical of many emerging into young adulthood, voiced the need for her parents to establish a new relationship with her.

Why do parents sometimes procrastinate in switching roles from controlling to supportive parents? There are a number of reasons, some conscious, some unconscious.

Some fear that letting their children go is an admission that they, the parents, are getting old. Becky, a student in a college class I attended, told of how her father's company always gave a Christmas dinner party for the families of the executives. Becky is eight and ten years older than her brother and sisters.

"The little kids were always allowed to go to the dinner," Becky said, "but I had to stay home. This year I insisted I go. Dad's colleagues expressed surprise when they met me. Their wives said to mother, 'We didn't know you had a daughter this age!' Mother was furious with me, because she had to face up to her age."

Some parents fear losing the attention, affection, and

assistance of their children.

"What can I do with my mother-in-law?" one young bride asked. "She calls every day. Her husband is often out of town on business, and she expects Dick, my husband, to come over and repair every leaky faucet or clogged drain or just come and talk to her—or rather, listen to her talk. I've been thinking we should move just far enough away so a telephone call would be a toll call."

Unconsciously, perhaps, this mother felt she should be rewarded by her son for her efforts when he was a child. When he was little, she had allowed him to absorb most of her time and money. Now she feared losing his attention and affection.

Not so Mrs. Cruse Blackburn of Southern California. Blind since she was three years old she had been dependent on her son, Raymond, since her husband died. But when Raymond wanted to marry, Cruse gladly released him. "God will have some way of looking after me," she said cheerfully. And she found that way.

### Children Will Make Mistakes

Some parents fear that the children, lacking good judgment, will make mistakes. Strange, isn't it, how we forget that one of the ways we learn is by making mistakes. Consider the attitude of the father in the story of the prodigal son in Luke 15. Surely his wise father-mind told him his son's request was foolish. But the father knew his son would have to learn some lessons on his own, and so he not only let his son go, but gave him his inheritance.

We forget also that God has given to each of us the *right* to make mistakes. A father who had suffered heartache from the waywardness of two of his children wrote: "Parents need to learn that there comes a time in the life of every person when he has a 'right to be wrong.' Development into maturity and independence involves decision making, and always carries with it the potential of error, whether deliberate or not. Thus to be human is to have the right to be wrong. This 'right' does not make a wrong decision right; neither does it absolve one from the consequences of wrong choices. But our children have the 'right to be right' and the 'right to be wrong.'"

### Reluctance of Children to Leave Parents

Sometimes the child is the one reluctant to break away from the parents. Then the parents must gently push the child from the nest.

Sharon was only nineteen when she wanted to get married. Her parents warned her there could be problems because her fiance', Steve, came from an entirely different background. Sharon didn't think there would be problems. Three months after the marriage Sharon showed up at home with tales of complaint against Steve.

"We think Steve is a fine young man, and evidently you do too, or you wouldn't have married him" her parents said and sent her back to Steve. And thus they nudged her from the nest when she wanted to crawl back in.

What then can we do to help our young people achieve liberation from complete dependence on us and develop into responsible adults?

1. *Constantly encourage them to become independent.*

Parents vary in the way in which they grant freedom to their children. Some are lenient when the children are young and then restrict and prohibit more and more as the children get older. Others maintain the same rules throughout childhood, adolescence, and even into adulthood. Still others apply the most restraints when the child is young and then little by little allow more and more freedom.

When the first method is followed, when children are clamped down on more and more as they get older and older, they are apt to erupt like volcanoes. On the other hand if the parents do not release their hold gradually, the children will feel insecure when they are pushed from the nest.

"My parents did everything for me until I graduated from high school. Then suddenly they told me I was on my own," one girl confided. "I was petrified. For weeks I couldn't sleep."

"I know," another one said, "only it happened to me when

I was 20. "'You're an adult now,' my parents said. Did they expect me suddenly to change overnight? If they had let me make decisions little by little and had reassured me of their help if I needed it, I would have felt much more secure."

Encouraging our eaglets to fly is a process usually requiring two decades or more in time and much love, sacrifice, patience, and understanding. When freedom is granted according to the responsibility shown, children grow and develop into independent young persons.

Actually parents know we never really are independent, but rather interdependent. Nature illustrates this interdependence in many ways. On a recent trip to the desert I learned of the help a yucca plant, called by the Spaniards "our Lord's candle," and an inconspicuous white moth give to each other.

The yucca blooms only at night. In the moonlight the moth flits to a blossom and gathers a ball of pollen. Then with her sharp, pointed oviposter—an egg-laying device—she stabs the pistil of the flower and deposits her eggs there at the same time as she rams the pollen down inside the pistil of the yucca, thus fertilizing the plant. In time the pollinated plant produces seeds. The moth larvae, still cradled in the seed pods of the tree, devour some of the seeds. Other seeds drop to the ground, and new yucca plants begin to grow. The larvae bore their way out of the seed pod, drop to the ground, spin cocoons around themselves and finally emerge as moths to carry on the cycle.

Parents need to remember that their children will realize this interdependence as they mature. But the road to learning the necessity and value of interdependence is often over the bumpy, uncomfortable road of independence. Consequently to rear children so they become self-reliant and independent is one of the primary and most important tasks of parents.

2. *Be patient and accepting even when you can't understand or agree with your children's behavior.*

They might not be as demonstrative of their love and affection as they were formerly. "Don't kiss me!" we'll hear, maybe even, "Don't touch me!" Their remarks might make us feel as though we have leprosy; but we shall have to remind ourselves that when our children utter these stay-away warnings, it isn't because they love us the less, but because they are trying to break their dependence on us. It may hurt when we see them pouring out their affection on their friends and even on older persons whom they have chosen to be their confidantes. The temptation might come to feel slighted, unloved, unappreciated, but we need to withstand the temptation to tears, complaining, or self-pity of any kind. We should not insist they show us affection, but instead rejoice that our children truly are maturing.

Growing children might not confide in us as much any more. "Don't ask me!" "Forget it!" "You wouldn't understand!" "Leave me alone, won't you?" Over and over parents may hear this. We need to respect this desire on their part for privacy and to work out things on their own.

One mother noticed how her adolescent daughter would begin to share with her and then abruptly stop. Finally she asked her daughter why she stopped. "Oh," said the girl shrugging, "it sounds silly when I say it. You wouldn't understand."

This sensitive woman had been bereaved of her mother in her teens. With no one to confide in she had poured out her woes into her diary. She had kept the diary. She dug it out now. "Maybe this would interest you," she said casually to her daughter who then confided in her mother more frequently.

If the young adult chooses not to confide, parents do well not to question, probe, or demand that they be told everything.

Young adults might exaggerate too. Go into your room and rock for a while in your rocking chair before you get furious about something they have said. Ask yourself if they have exaggerated for effect's sake.

A friend of mine told of overhearing a telephone conversation of her daughter.

"Oh, your mom got all upset, did she?" Silence. "That's too bad." Silence. "My Mom? Naw, she knows I mean only a fourth of what I say."

*Well,* thought that mother, *I hadn't known that before, but*

*I'm sure glad to learn it now.*

Children's grooming habits frequently irritate their elders. When young people choose to dress and groom themselves in a different fashion, parents protest, explode, ridicule, demand reformation, suffer in martyr-like silence, and ignore, not only the style of dress, but also the young person. They resign themselves to it or strike a compromise. Some parents adopt the youthful fashions themselves to the amusement of their friends. Perhaps the happiest route lies in recognizing that both parents and children have *rights*.

After a year away from home Tom moved back to attend a community college. "The casual—he called it!—dress was hard for us to accept," his mother confessed. "His long, unkempt hair particularly annoyed my fastidious husband. Finally my husband said, 'Look, son, I can stand to sit and look across the table at long hair, but I can't stand it when it's uncombed. Either comb it or eat your meals on a tray in your room.' Tom sputtered and then began to comb his hair."

Our children might not adopt our values. "What do you do," a tall, graying, highly intelligent father asked, "if your children scorn and ridicule what you hold dear?" He was touching on what can be a very sore point, especially for fathers.

The wrong reaction, of course, is to despair. True, when a father cannot look at his children and see in them that which satisfies him, and when he feels completely helpless and frustrated in doing anything about this, he is tempted to despair. He may mask his despair with disgust—or a thousand little disgusts, expressed toward the child. The child, it seems, no longer can do anything to please the father. In some cases the father may revert to sulking and acting like a selfish child himself. More seriously, he may identify with his child, against his own convictions, and pretend to adopt his child's standards and philosophies as his own, when, in reality, they are not. But when a middle-aged person reverts to adolescent behavior or thought, it works havoc with his integrity.

What *can* parents do? In the first place, we need to re-examine what we claim to be our set of values and the actual way in which we live our lives. We cannot hold double standards. As our children observe day by day how we live and talk and act, they will pick up the values we model. We cannot say to our children, "Don't drink. Don't smoke," if we drink and smoke. When we want them to show appreciation and gratitude, we need to ask ourselves, "Do they see me expressing appreciation?" If we want them to be free of the lust for money and material things, we shall have to examine ourselves as to how much desire for these actually do control our lives. *Why* are we working? So in some cases, if we see our children adopting values with which we are not happy, we may have to say, "I'm going to stop some of the crazy things I've been doing." If they adopt values different from ours, we may have to be humble enough to ask, "Who is choosing more wisely, they or we?"

3. *Maintain an attitude of love and trust rather than of guilt and worry.*

Many parents suffer guilt because they wonder if they raised their children in the right way.

"We had five children," one woman said, "and they were just far enough apart in years so all five have been brought up in a different way, depending on which method of child rearing was in vogue when the child was born. Goodness knows which method was best, or if any of them were any good."

There's little point in fretting about the past. If you did your best, leave it in God's hands. He has a way of compensating for our mistakes.

But what do you do when you *know* you've made mistakes in raising your children?

"I came to know Christ only a couple of years ago," a mother said. "If I had known him earlier, I would have taught my children altogether different values."

The answer is, live Christ now. Your children will see the difference he has made in you.

"I've been a Christian all our married life," another mother said, "but that doesn't mean I've done everything right. I sometimes became very irritated and even angry with my children. Sometimes I punished them unjustly. When I think of it, I feel so guilty."

How good it is to know that not only does God forgive us, but he also enables our children to recover from injury and to make adjustments. As Reuel Howe expressed in his book *The Creative Years*, "the mistakes we make are not nearly as powerful as the love we give."

Many parents today are struggling with guilt feelings as their children give birth to babies out of wedlock or divorce after only a few years of married life. "What did we do wrong?" they cry.

Maybe nothing. We need to remember that though we can influence and guide, the final choice rests with our children. As we said before, we have to give our children the same right God gives us, the right to choose.

But if we are not to feel guilty, what should be our response to a child who has deeply hurt us?

The father of a child who first informed her parents she was a lesbian and was killed later in a shoot-out, said:

> The Christian parent will continue to hold on to his or her child, come what may, with the bonds of faithful love. Parents can perhaps, if they wish, permit the hard experiences of life to 'kill' their love for a child who has spitefully used them. But, conversely, they can, if they will, continue to love that wayward individual in the hope (maybe it will prove vain) that he or she will some day respond and that some day reconciliation will occur.
>
> Parents with a Christian perspective know something about the unselfishness of the love of God for his wayward children. Such was the love which prompted him to send to earth his Redeemer-Son and which moves his Spirit to work continuingly in his erring children for their forgiveness and spiritual growth. This is the kind of love which Christians are exhorted to reveal in their dealings with other people: pure, unselfish love, never achieved by humans fully but always worth the effort. The forgiven— unto seventy times seven—are in turn forgivers—unto seventy times seven.

"Joan came home five months pregnant," one mother said.

"She wanted to keep her baby, but neither the boy who was the baby's father or she wanted to marry. We were crushed. What were we to do? The baby was born, a beautiful, healthy child. Now Joan wants to go back to college and make something of her life. I'm caring for the baby. Of course, I wish circumstances had been diffeent, but I'm rather enjoying having a baby to care for again. And Joan loves her baby dearly, because she feels God used the whole circumstance to help her get right with him and get her values straightened out."

"To love at all is to be vulnerable," C. S. Lewis observed in *The Four Loves.* He wrote:

> Love anything, and your heart will certainly be wrung and possibly be broken. If you want to make sure of keeping it intact, you must give your heart to no one, not even to an animal. Wrap it carefully round with hobbies and little lux-uries; avoid all entanglements; lock it up safe in the casket or coffin of your selfishness. But in that casket—safe, dark, motionless, airless—it will change. It will not be broken; it will become unbreakable, impenetrable, irredeemable . . . . The only place outside Heaven where you can be perfectly safe from all the dangers of love is Hell.

"I was heartbroken when Annie told me she was pregnant," another mother, herself a widow, confessed. "But how could I turn Annie out on the street? A short while later I came down with an illness that kept me in bed for months and months. How grateful I was for Annie's loving care of me. The baby was born. I recovered and went back to work. What a treat it was to come home every evening to a sparkling house, a hot dinner, laundry done and a cooing grandson! Now that he is older we have him in a Christian nursery, and Annie is back at college. We're believing roses will bloom out of the ashes."

When a divorced daughter or son comes home with small children and all the attendant problems, parents find them-selves really cast on God to understand what is the Christian way to respond. They forgive, love, and accept, yes—but does their responsibility end with this, or are they expected to raise another family just when they were looking forward to years of more freedom? How good that God has promised us wisdom, each of us in our individual, differing situations.

Another heartbreaking situation arises when children leave or run away from home and never contact their parents. Then to hang on in love and trust is an acid test. The parents will be tempted to think the child cherishes no love or gratitude towards them at all. At times like this we need to cling to the fact that it is almost impossible to kill a child's love for his parents.

"It's an odd psychological fact," a counselor at a home for juvenile delinquent boys told me, "but boys who have nothing to go back to at all get really homesick and want to return home."

Now if this is true for children who have been mistreated, how much stronger must be the love ties where the home atmosphere has been warm and accepting.

Allowing children to explore their dreams calls for willingness to let the child experiment and suffer and fail—or, happily, succeed.

"Our son thinks he is going to be the great American novelist. His wife was more interested in a home and family than in being poor. Their marriage lasted two years. Now our son has taken off for Europe. He says he is going to gather material for his book. I don't know what to say to him," a mother confided. "When his father was his age he said he was going to be an artist. Instead he settled for teaching. He has enjoyed it too, I think. He has always said he'd get back to his art after he retired. I wonder if that will be too late . . . . It's hardest when our son needs money. It's not that we don't have it to give. But should we? Or should we let him try to get along on his own and find out if he really can earn a living writing? If he tries and fails, at least he'll have the satisfaction of knowing he has tried."

Parents, of course, will want to remember their children about whom they are concerned, in prayer to God. As we pray it is helpful to form a mental image of the kind of persons we desire them to become—and hopefully we have let God shape these desires. Focus on that image. See them in your mind's eye.

Thank God that this will be so. And then begin to treat your young persons as the responsible individuals you believe they will become.

4. *Above all, don't let relationships rupture.*

Emily, a mother of several young adult children, tells her story.

"Virginia was dating a divorced man considerably older than she. He had custody of the two children from his previous marriage. Other factors caused us concern also. Their racial and cultural backgrounds were very different. We talked and talked with Virginia. Our concerns got us no place. So we prayed God would stop the marriage. But though I prayed and prayed, I could get no assurance God would answer my prayer. My frustration mounted. The relationship with our daughter worsened to the point where Virginia moved out. I continued to pray. Finally it occurred to me I should change my prayer. I began to pray that the good relationship we had enjoyed with Virginia before would be restored. Immediately I was assured I was praying for the right thing. My attitude changed, and Virginia's did also. We were reconciled. In the end she did marry, and the marriage is a happy one. Her husband has become a dedicated Christian, and our relationships have never been better."

Walls often come between parents and children when the young people go away to college, especially if neither parents or children write or call.

"Our son never writes," a troubled mother told me. "He used to call collect. Last time when he did, his father asked him why he didn't write. Joe said there wasn't anything that would interest us. That really made my husband blow up. He told me not to accept any more pay calls from him."

"And you?"

Her eyes dropped to the floor. "I've stopped writing too."

"But you're unhappy about it?"

"Of course. He's coming home in a couple weeks' time for Christmas, and his father is ready to blister him."

Here is a situation where the parents can determine the

future of their relationship with their child. Being a parent calls for infinite patience. Sometimes we need to go, not only the second mile, but the third, and fourth too. A guiding question to ask ourselves is, what can I do in order that the relationship between our child and us be the best it can possibly be? If we keep in view our ultimate goal, a continuing good relationship with our child, it will help us see present difficulties in perspective, and we shall discover we can afford to be generous and forgiving. Time matures all of us. With maturity comes a different point of view. Sometimes it takes longer for some to mature than others. Then we have to wait. And show *our* maturity.

The father of an able, young doctor tells of how when his son left for college, he tossed him a couple of rolled up dollars. "If you need me, call," he said. And he did. Years later, the night of the boy's wedding, as the son was saying goodbye to his father, he handed his dad two dollars. The father fingered them, then with a smile handed them back. A few weeks later the son bumped into a problem and called his father. "I don't think that would have happened," the father said, "if the dollars hadn't kept the way open all the previous years."

It will be worth every effort to maintain good relationships with our children. We cannot emphasize strongly enough that *in the years ahead we shall need them and they will need us.*

5. *Be thankful for the help others give.*

We are not alone. Good teachers play an important role. A trusted pastor can become a true friend. Our young adult children may seek out other older adults to whom they feel free to confide, at least for a time. Don't be jealous of these relationships. Welcome them. Encourage them. Others can make our jobs easier.

6. *Remember that in the end our children are God's.*

Have we given them to him? We can trust him and never give up hope. We love and care, but God loves and cares infinitely more.

7. *Appreciate them.*

Appreciate them for the joy, freshness, and vigor they bring to a home. Appreciate them for the help their strong, young arms and untiring bodies can give. Appreciate them for their skills and abilities manifested in song and music, in art and crafts, in baking, cooking and sewing, in carpentry and painting. Appreciate them for their warm love for Jesus, for kindnesses they show others, for compassion. Appreciate them for their keen discernment, their glowing idealism. Appreciate them for their knowledgeable conversation, spiked with humor and colorful language, seasoned with a reflected thought you wouldn't have thought them capable of yet. Appreciate them for the loyal, clear-eyed friendship they offer you. Appreciate them when they correct you or point out your inconsistencies. Appreciate them for being themselves, unique, marvelous individuals. Appreciate them, and in your bedroom at night, as you and your mate share the joy they have brought you, smile in the dark and say, "How could we ever have brought such lovely persons into being?"

As your heart is warmed, you will discover a wonderful miracle taking place. *You* are being appreciated.

My husband, while speaking at a conference, was staying in a private home. One morning Luverne came into the living room to find the father vigorously blowing his nose. "Read this," he said, handing a letter to my husband. "It's from Carol. She's at college."

The letter read in part:

Dear Ones,

I may not have been the best correspondent this year, but I want you all to know that each year I am away, you become dearer to me. I love you for what you are and what you have helped me become. For our wonderful closeness of family ties, I am very grateful. . . . For all your warmth and sincerity, for the love you've given so freely, for the happy and trying times we've shared, for everything you are and represent to me in high ideals and fine living, for the joy of being part of such a wonderful family, I thank our Father above! Not only now, but always, you are in my heart, because you are part of me.

With tenderness,
Carol

As we genuinely appreciate our young people and express our appreciation, a bonus for them will be the flowering of self-confidence. They will need self-confidence. They will need to be assured they are of value, that they can find their place in society and become contributing members, that they can control the controllable factors in life and make peace with the uncontrollable. They will need this if they are going to take wings and fly, to swoop and soar and rise above the problems of our troubled old world.

As helpers and guides, acknowledging our common humanity and weaknesses, mutually turning to God from whom all love and faith come, we as parents in our middle years can work for new relationships that will encourage our eaglets to fly.

## For Thought, Reflection, and Discussion

1. How would I rate my relationship with each of our children now?

very good        good                acceptable
could be better  strained            broken

2. What can I do specifically to improve relationships with each one?

3. Below is a list of things we say that block communication. Of which ones have I been guilty?

Stop that! (Ordering, commanding)
You should. You ought. (Admonishing)
You made a mistake! (Judging)
What you need to know is . . . (Using logic)
Lazy. Selfish. Stupid. Idiot. (Name calling)
You feel this way because . . . (Interpreting)
Who? What? When? Why? Where? (Probing)
Don't worry, everything will work out (Reassuring)
I'll tell you what to do (Advising)

When I was your age (Setting one's self up as example)

4. What is meant by becoming involved on an emotional level when we listen?

5. How can we tune into feelings behind words?

6. What have I found helpful to enable me to concentrate on my child's point of view and his or her emotional distress?

7. What nonverbal clues can help me understand my child?

8. What principles of communication do we find in these Bible verses?

Proverbs 18:13; James 1:19a.

Proverbs 29:20; 21:23; James 1:19.

James 5:16.

Proverbs 17:9b, Galatians 6:1, 1 Thessalonians 5:11, Romans 14:13.

Philippians 2:1–4, Ephesians 4:2.

Ephesians 4:15, 25, Colossians 3:9.

Proverbs 15:1, 14:29, 25:15, 29:11.

Philippians 3:13.

Colossians 3:13, Proverbs 17:9, 1 Peter 4:8, Ephesians 4:32.

Ephesians 4:31, Proverbs 17:14, Romans 13:13.

If your children are still teenagers you may enjoy Haim G. Ginott's book *Between Parent and Teenager.*

# The Last Harvest:
# Caring for Aging Parents

*Kindness should begin at home, supporting needy parents. This is something that pleases God very much.*
—1 Timothy 5:4 (Living Bible)

Phyllis handed a gaily checked apron to her mother.

"Busy day ahead," she said briskly. "Wash and dry the dishes. Put them away. Guests are coming tonight. We'll go to the market. Later you can make a cole slaw for dinner."

Phyllis' mother responded with a smile and hummed as she washed the dishes. Phyllis brought an armful of laundry from her mother's room and loaded the washer. She tapped her mother on the shoulder and smiled. "Time for the first walk of the day," she reminded, motioning toward the bathroom. *With guests coming tonight I'll have to be especially mindful today and remind her,* Phyllis thought, *and I'll have to check for unintentional messes.*

Dishes done, the two drove to a shopping center. After the marketing Phyllis remembered she had a check to cash. "Wait in the car," she said to her mother. "I'll be right back."

The lines in the bank were longer than Phyllis had expected. As she stood waiting a woman came up to her. "Was it your mother waiting for you in the car? She's wandering around, looking for you."

"Oh, no!" Phyllis exclaimed and dashed out to find her mother wandering aimlessly about on the parking lot.

"I was looking for Henry," her mother said. "Henry took me to the store and then he went off and left me."

*I won't be able to leave her any more*, Phyllis thought on the way home.

At home Phyllis shampooed and set her mother's hair. She phoned then for the sitter for her mother they would need Thursday night when they went out. After her mother's nap Phyllis helped her mother bathe and laid out the clothes her mother would be wearing for dinner.

That evening after the guests had gone, in the refuge of their bedroom, Phyllis collapsed on her husband's shoulder.

"It isn't that I don't love mother and want to care for her," her words were muffled. "It's just that it's not always easy. If she's going to keep in touch with reality, she needs to be with people. But tonight especially it was hard including her in the conversation. After I had had her tell Mrs. Brooks how she makes her cole slaw—and mother's cole slaw is delicious—I was at a loss to know what other subjects to introduce." She blew her nose and straightened. "And then you came home the last minute and told me two extra guests were coming, and I had pie only for six. I wanted to tell you right then and there how upsetting this is for me. But I didn't dare. Not in front of mother. She might misunderstand and think *she* had done something to upset me."

"You can tell me off now," her husband said grinning.

"That's the trouble," Phyllis was laughing and crying. "I don't feel like doing it now!!"

Phyllis' situation is typical of many middle-aged children who have loved and cared about their parents and who now, at a time in life when they had looked forward to a little freedom, find themselves having to care *for* their parents. Even though love is there, tensions are inevitable.

Tensions between middle-aged children and their aging parents seem to be most acute when: (1) the children have lived most of their adult life in the city while the parents have remained on the farm; (2) the children are second generation citizens of this land and the parents are immigrants; (3) and when the children have become so well educated and risen to such a high social strata that they do not want to be associated with their parents any more.

Difficulties can arise also because 25 years have lapsed usually, since the time the children broke away and formed their own home and the time when some of the children receive the aging parents into their home to care for them. People change during the years.

Occasionally also mother and daughter or father and son or mother-in-law and daughter-in-law or father-in-law and son-in-law compete with each other. Stress then is pronounced.

It also is difficult if there is difference in emphasis on authoritarianism and permissiveness, and this is especially true if there are grandchildren in the home.

But in spite of these problems most people feel responsible to care for their aging parents, according to their various needs. What does this involve? What needs do aging parents have?

Basic needs are: a home to live in, freedom to fill their time as they wish, and children who love and care.

## Helping Provide a Home

Generally people stay happier and healthier in their own homes (though there are always exceptions to this). If they need help to continue living in their own homes, children can help in a number of ways;

—by hiring someone to do weekly cleaning or laundry or yard work

—by bringing over hot meals or arranging for meals on wheels

—by helping with repairs, window washing, putting up storm windows (if the house is old)

—by installing a telephone by their bed, then having someone call them regularly

—by helping with grocery shopping and transportation

—by arranging for a home health aide to call if this is needed

—by visiting regularly or writing or calling

—by supplying things they use and need regularly if their budget is limited

—by showing affection

A friend of mine, Hazel, found many ways to care lovingly for her invalid mother when she chose to stay on in their own home. Fortunately Hazel's father was exceptionally skilled in giving his wife nursing care, and this was a big help. But with the exception of times when they were out of town Hazel went every day for six years to visit her mother. She did her laundry, ran errands, shopped, shampooed and set her mother's hair or took her to a beauty shop, baked and cooked for her mother and her father.

"I was happy to do it," my friend insists. "Caring for mother was a rewarding experience. To begin with I wondered where I would find time to do all the extras. I have an active family and handle the office work of my husband's business. But God always gave me strength, patience, and the listening capacity needed."

If your parents want to move to another part of the country, suggest they rent first. They should make sure they like the new setting before they settle there permanently.

If aging parents want to move out of their own home and live somewhere else other than with you, there are many alternatives to explore:

—motor homes in which to travel

—mobile homes, stationary in courts

—apartment hotels (some operated by churches)

—retirement villages, self-governing, complete with churches, banks, hospital, doctors' building, golf course, restaurants, shops and recreation facilities.

—board and care homes

—private retirement homes

—retirement homes operated by churches

—public housing for low-income persons

—private homes.

For information on low cost financing available through

the Department of Housing and Urban Development, write to them at Washington, D.C. Public housing for older persons varies from attached one-story buildings to high-rise structures. Most apartments are either studio apartments or one-bedroom. Safety equipment is provided as well as laundry rooms and some recreational facilities. Rents are based on ability to pay.

If your parents have come to the place where they can no longer carry on independently and you are wondering what to do, answering the following questions might shed some light as to what course you should follow. Ask yourself:

1. How much will they let me do? Will they let me make plans for them?
2. How much can they do for themselves?
3. How much can they afford?
4. How much can we afford?
5. What are we able to do for them? How is our health? What demands does our work place on us?
6. Would we be able to get along together if we lived together?
7. Would they like to live where we live and would they like our way of living?
8. Are the plans that we are considering ones that we can follow for several years?

If parents and children find it difficult to get along when they live together, can arrangement be made for the parents to live with someone else? Sometimes this works out better.

And what shall we do if the day comes when they need a nursing home? So many critical articles have been written on nursing homes that a negative public attitude has been created. Because of this many people are living alone in misery, afraid that a nursing home might be even worse. Relatives of those who live in nursing homes often suffer needlessly from a sense of guilt. As one director of retirement homes confesses, "Certainly there are people in nursing homes who are miserable, but this is also true of those in hospitals. The fact is these people are less miserable and have a better chance for a brighter future because of the nursing home. In many nursing homes fantastic progress is being made, not only in the quality of nursing care but in the area of spiritual and social components of care."

Another director said: "If physical care makes life possible, psycho-social care makes life worthwhile," and added that it is this aspect that is being emphasized especially in homes sponsored by churches.

Typical of life-care facilities where one can advance from one level of care to another as health dictates is the Good Samaritan Village in Hastings, Nebraska. This bustling retirement center houses almost 1300 residents. The village, located on 90 acres, has more than 700 apartment units, paved streets and sidewalks, all utilities and even a small lake. Seven levels provide care for the residents: one-, two- or three-bedroom apartment units, for self-sustaining couples or individuals; similar apartment units for those who can maintain their own household with some assistance from a house visitor; accommodations for those who need a meal a day served to them in the common dining room or brought to them in their apartments; facilities for couples who can no longer maintain their own households; care homes for people who are up and about but need supervision and meals; and the infirmary for those in wheelchairs or walkers or in need of total bed care.

The Good Samaritan Village is administered by the Evangelical Lutheran Good Samaritan Society, with home offices in Sioux Falls, South Dakota. The Society tends to emphasize smaller, more home-like units in neighborhoods where the retired people have spent their lives, but they do have some larger facilities like the one in Hastings.

The Evangelical Covenant Church of America operates sixteen life-care centers and practically every other denomination also sponsors this type of housing for senior citizens.

The waiting list at church-sponsored homes, however, often is long, so if you can anticipate your needs, get your name on the waiting list early.

In addition to church-sponsored homes, there are many excellent private homes.

If you are considering a retirement center for your parents

or choosing a home for them, it might be helpful to consider these points:

1. Is it clean? well-ventilated? well-lighted?
2. Ask to see a week's menu.
3. Is medical care available?
4. Become acquainted with those operating the home.
5. Is it near churches, shopping, etc.?
6. Do guests have freedom?
7. If your parent is single, will your parent have a room alone or have to share?
8. Does the home provide entertainment or recreation?
9. May the residents have guests?
10. What does it cost?

If you are considering taking your parents into your home, you may find it helpful to consult some of the books listed at the end of this chapter.

## Work and Happiness

How much work do older people need in order to be happy? The answer, of course, is that this will vary with different people.

There will be differences even among older people who can look back on their lives with contentment and satisfaction. Some will want to pack their calendars full. "We're busier than ever," they say happily. Others cherish their newly-granted freedom from a busy schedule.

Ambitious, achievement-oriented people usually fear aging and can't tolerate the idea of not working. "I'm not retired," one insisted, "I'm re-fired." "So long as you keep busy you'll be all right," others say. For them work is exceedingly important in order to retain a sense of self-esteem.

People who have been dependent on others for one thing or another will feel minimum need for activity. Typical of these is the man who has let his wife do all the talking and decision-making and the healthy woman who has done little else than satisfy her physical and social needs. Aging for them tends to produce apathy.

Yet another type are those persons whom old age finds becoming more and more disorganized and confused.

So happiness in the declining years seems to depend, at least to a significant degree, on whether our activities develop out of healthy needs and interests and continue to bring satisfaction. For some persons retirement can be tolerated only if they can continue to find work where they can use their skills. Others welcome the opportunity to develop new interests and skills. Some relish social isolation and bask in freedom from pressure and responsibility. Others go crazy with isolation and "nothing to do."

Final decisions as to what to do and how to do are Mom and Dad's privilege. They know best what they enjoy doing and want to do. Goodness knows, at this time in life the last thing they need is someone to boss them around. Nor do they want charity. Or fuss. Or condescension.

It isn't easy for children to know how to strike the balance between helping and granting freedom. We run the risk of hurting them and ourselves in the process, but as always in life we do the best we can.

At the same time that parents want freedom, we need to remember that none of us ever out-live the need to be needed. Our parents have been needed for a very long time. To feel no longer needed can be grievous indeed for them. We hear now and again of people who die very soon after retiring, quite possibly because they do not feel needed any longer and so see no purpose in living. Surely parents should never have to out-live the realization that their family still needs them. And without question nothing is more painful than for parents to pick up the message from their children that they are no longer needed. Some children, aware that this would be hurtful, try to pretend a need of their parents. But do we have to counterfeit our need? We *do* need them and will need them as long as they live.

Our children need our parents too. Grandparents are their tie with a past about which they know little but from which they can learn much.

This does not mean, however, that our parents have

authority over us or our children. All that is needed is for them to be what they are, our fathers and mothers, our own flesh and blood, our ties with the past. At the same time we need to remember always that they need to feel we need them, they need to be assured that they have children who love and care for and about them.

## Children Who Love and Care

How do we say "I love you" to our parents?

An ancient letter shows us. It describes an unusual love affair. The chief character in the story is a wizened, scarred, aging man. He can't even support his beloved; in fact, his beloved is supporting him. He is, you see, a prisoner.

His affair is not just with one woman either, but rather with some touchy, quarrelsome, independent women, and also with some men.

The love affair is being sustained through letters, for lover and beloved are separated by many miles. One of these letters has been preserved for us. We know it as the epistle Paul wrote to the congregation at Philippi, and it is to this letter we turn now to learn how to say, "I love you."

1. *Say it.*

To say, "Of course they know I love them," is not enough. Paul reveals his affection for the Philippians in his letter. "I hold you in my heart," he writes. And again, "I yearn for you." "My beloved." "My brethren, whom I love and long for."

When we are not limited to communicating through letters and phone or tape, we can say, "I love you," not only with words, but also by touch and tender looks. Put your arms around your aging parents. Hug them. Hold them close. Stroke their hair. Kiss them. Joke with them. Tease them gently and lovingly.

2. *Love, not only in word, but also in deed.*

In the case of Paul and the Philippian Christians the love between them was not simply an exchange of sentimental words either. Paul had suffered to see the Philippian Christians introduced to God.

They, in turn, tried to understand Paul's needs. Even Paul

struggled with balancing his budget. The Christians at Philippi offered to help. Usually Paul preferred paying his own way, but he felt so close to the Philippians that he accepted their help.

At the time he wrote this letter Paul was an imprisoned man. Some Bible scholars think respected prisoners like him were not put behind bars but rather confined to a house. For Paul this very likely meant renting a house. The Philippian congregation sent money to Paul to help him meet his needs. They also had a congregational meeting and elected one, Epaphroditus, to go and be with Paul. Money could help pay the rent and buy groceries, but feet and hands were needed to bring the groceries home. A cheerful, courageous heart was needed even more, to encourage the aging Paul.

Our gift-giving to our aging parents should be equally thoughtful. For many years my mother pleaded with us not to buy any more "things." "The house is full," she explained. "there's no room to put any more." But she welcomed shrubs and flowers for her garden, an airplane ticket to visit us, trips to new, unexplored or old familiar places. Mother also loved to entertain—even at 80 plus—and one year my sister-in-law gave her a big box of gaily decorated napkins for all occasions, much to her delight. Another child in the family had a telephone installed by her bed so she wouldn't have to run down the stairs to answer it if it rang while she was upstairs.

3. *Express appreciation to your parents for all they have done and meant to you.*

Gratefully Paul acknowledges the gifts from the Philippians. "I am thankful for your partnership," he wrote. "It was kind of you to share my trouble." "The gifts you sent were a fragrant offering."

What do you appreciate most about your parents? As a young person I was restless, and my wanderings took me far from home. One day 2,000 miles away from home, my heart welled up with love for my father and appreciation for all he had meant to me. Impulsively I sat down and wrote a letter, pouring out my heart. When he received it, mother told me later, Dad read and reread it. And then, holding it in his hand, he said, "We should frame this." A few months later my father was disabled with a heart attack. By the time I reached home he was conscious only long enough for us to exchange a few words before he died. I've always been glad I wrote that letter.

4. *Try to understand what is important to your parents.*

The Philippian Christians understood that not only material things were important to Paul. He admonished the Philippians, "stand firm in the Lord." They fulfilled Paul's desire. They stood firm. And they were successful also in keeping their children true to the Lord and passing on to them their own gracious spirit of hospitality.

How do we know this? Sixty years later a Christian, Ignatius, passed through Philippi on his way to martyrdom at Rome. At the time he was a "wanted person." To give him asylum was dangerous. But the Philippian Christians ran the risk and took him in. Later Polycarp wrote to the Philippian Christians commending them for their action. It is the one letter of Polycarps that has been preserved for us. But because we have that letter we know that two generations after Paul this church was still standing firm and was still manifesting the spirit of love, generosity, and hospitality that had characterized it from the beginning.

What is important to your parents? That the family name continue to be held in high esteem? That family solidarity continue? Has your father been a career man in the service of his country? Is devotion to his country still important to him? Have your parents worked hard to support certain philanthropic causes? Have they been Christians, concerned that their children lead godly lives?

As you consider their interests and concerns, is there anything you can do to perpetuate them? Aging persons need to feel, not only that they have made a contribution to society, but that their influence will continue to be felt.

5. *Build and nourish confidence and faith.*

Paul's strong confidence and faith in what God could do for the Philippians is echoed again and again in the letter.

"I am sure he who began a good work in you will bring it

to completion," he reassures them. "God is at work in you, both to will and to work." "Let those of us who are mature be thus minded; and if in anything you are otherwise minded, God will reveal that to you also." "My God will supply every need of yours."

Aging parents need to have their faith and trust nourished and strengthened. The death of friends and relatives and their own failing health and declining strength will remind them that death, the ultimate, final test, is drawing near. To face death courageously and cheerfully calls for faith, confidence, and assurance.

We can help our parents build faith. If we haven't done so previously, and if we are uncertain about their relationship with God, we can talk with them about this.

If they need transportation, we can make arrangements so they can get to worship services. We can read and pray with them and give them books, records and tapes, as we see they will be used and appreciated. As we reminisce with them over all the way God has led and cared for us, we can reassure one another that God will continue to care for us, and will not forsake us. All of us, no matter how strong we have been, need this ministry of encouragement and faith-building from others. Our parents perhaps were the first ones to teach us to trust in God. Now, in gratitude, we can reach out in love and strengthen their faith and confidence in God.

As our trust in God grows, peace and joy will garrison our hearts. Read through the epistle to the Philippians and count how many times the word *joy* and *rejoice* appear. Remember these expressions of joy came from a man chained to a guard day and night, from one who never knew when the summons to death would come. But he could rejoice because he was assured of God's love. He knew of God's love through the death of God's son on the cross, true, but he also experienced God's love through the Philippian Christians. When trials and troubles come, we may always be assured, through God's Word, of his love and support. But it surely helps when others also tell us they love and care. God loves people through people. God can love our aging parents through us. We need to demonstrate our love to them and to express our appreciation of their valuable contributions to life. Let's seek to support the things they have held dear. Finally, and perhaps most significantly, let's reaffirm our faith in God and help them build confidence and faith in our loving, faithful God.

**Broken Relationships**

People sometimes carry over into their middle years re-sentments and ill feelings toward their parents which have smouldered since childhood and which hinder happy relation-ships. A friend of mine tells how this resentment was for her.

"I had every reason to be happy with a thoughtful husband who provided well for us, three lovely children and a beautiful home, yet I wasn't. I cried every day. I didn't know why.

"One day my pastor noticed my despondency, but I wasn't ready to talk. Three weeks passed. My tears and depression became so bad that finally I went to see the pastor. We talked for three hours, and I cried the whole time.

"He asked me to pray that God would reveal to me my problem. I was to come back in a week's time.

"As I prayed, the mistreatment I had received from my father during childhood and my resulting hatred of him kept coming back to mind.

"When I went back, the pastor asked if anything had been revealed to me. I said yes, but I couldn't tell him about it. Then all of a sudden I burst into tears and sobbed out the whole story. From that moment my attitude towards my father changed. I went home happier than I could ever remember being. Compas-sion, forgiveness, and love for my father began to flow into my heart. So great was the change that the pastor could see it written all over my face when I went to see him again.

"God's Spirit had to change my feelings. I couldn't change them on my own. Through God's grace I was able to write to my father and tell him I loved him and ask him to forgive me for all the ill feelings I had cherished against him. I began to pray that my parents would have this same relationship with

God that had become mine.

"A few years later my parents came to visit us. I was able to really talk to my father for the first time. I told mother how God had helped me and how personal he had become to me, how he had cleansed me of past sin, given me a new nature, and made me a new person in Christ. Before my mother left to return home, she made a commitment to Christ. Now she is growing in faith.

"I wish I could say that my father has changed too, but so far he hasn't. We've had long talks. God has healed my memories, and I feel no ill toward Dad now, only love. If God has done this for me, I'm sure he can set Dad free too. So I continue to pray for him."

When family relationships are not what they should be, one warning signal may be our own inner unhappiness and depression. Resentment and anger, even when suppressed, drain us emotionally, leaving us dry and empty. When we overspend our emotional energy, depression often follows. When depression persists, we do well to ask ourselves first what has drained me emotionally? As we trust the Holy Spirit, things will be brought to mind we may have forgotten. It might be a fractured relationship which needs to be mended.

Unfortunately, we often have to be desperate before we are ready to take action. When my friend's pastor first asked her what was troubling her, she was not ready. Three more miserable weeks had to pass before she was willing to be helped.

The first glimmer of light came when she was able to pinpoint the cause of the broken relationship. She felt her basic problem was lack of love for her father. Instinctively she realized when she asked him for forgiveness, she must be careful not to blame him—though she could have. She knew she must not say, "I'm sorry I cherished such resentments toward you, *but* really you were very mean to me and mistreated me horribly." Instead she said simply, "God has shown me how wrong it has been on my part not to love you. I want to ask you to forgive me."

Sensitivity. Patience. Wisdom. Love. Willingness to help and willingness on our part to be helped by God. All of these we need as we care about and care for our aging parents. As we care for them, we can bear in mind that in this area too we are setting examples, laying patterns. Some day *we* will be the aging parents. The care we receive then may well be the kind of care we give now.

## For Reflection and Discussion

1. What changes might take place in the next five years that would affect my relationship with my parents?

2. If this should happen, what might be some of the options to meet new needs?

3. How would these various choices be viewed by my children? By my sisters and brothers? By my parents' friends? By my friends?

4. What am I doing to keep communication between my parents and me open and good?

5. Have my feelings toward and my relationship with my parents changed as I have seen them aging? If so, how?

6. What *is* my responsibility toward my parents?

7. How can I help my parents maintain good health and well-being?

8. What can I do if I see my parents are no longer able to handle money and transactions responsibly? Who can help deal with this problem?

9. How can I help my parents deal with loss of hearing, vision or other impairment?

10. What are some of the causes of senility? If this happens to my parents what can I do?

11. How can I deal with my concerns for my parents in regard to marriage, dating, or remarrying?

## Resource Books

*You and Your Aging Parent* by Barbara Silverstone, Helen Kandel Hyman, Pantheon Books, 1982. Helpful reading if you are considering moving your parents into your home.

*Ministry With the Aging* by William M. Clements, Harper and Row, 1981.

*Aging is a Family Affair* by Victoria E. Bumagin and Kathryn F. Him, Thomas Y. Crowell, 1979.

*The Harvard Medical School Health Letter Book* by Timothy G. Johnson and Stephen E. Goldfinger, Harvard University Press, 1981.

*Your Aging Parents* by Margaret J. Anderson, Concordia Publishing House, 1979.

*When Your Parents Grow Old* by Jane Otten and Florence D. Shelley, a Signet book, a reprint of a hardcover edition published by Thomas Y. Crowell Company, Inc.

*Home Care* by Florine DuFresne, Brethren Press, 1983. Practical suggestions if a parent is bedridden.

## 8

## Trees That Stand Alone

*To be free, to be able to stand up and leave everything behind—without looking back. To say Yes.*
—Dag Hammarskjold

Emerging as a rapidly growing minorities community in the western world are the singles: the single-singles or those who have never married, the separated, divorced, or deserted, the unwed mothers and fathers, and the widows and widowers. Life for many of them is bitterly difficult. They face snarled problems: financial, legal, social and personal.

Whether divorced, widowed, or never married, many singles find themselves wrestling with problems for which they had little or no preparation.

### Problems of the Divorced or Widowed

*Emotional Stability.* The emotional upheaval of divorce and bereavement rips them open. One woman, describing her divorce said: "I felt so fragile, like an open, walking sore." Another, three years after her divorce, simply shook her head and said, "It's still too painful to talk about."

"I knew there would be problems," admitted a mother of three, whose former husband was an alcoholic, "but I never dreamed they would be as critical or overwhelming. At times I've been tempted to despair."

*Financial Difficulty.* Almost all families who lose a parent find their expenses climb and their income drops. "Financially, it's disaster!" one mother of three, living in an older tract suburban house, declared. The sweep of her arm indicated the worn furnishings. "I don't know when we'll ever be able to replace this furniture. We should move into a new home. This house and neighborhood are rapidly deteriorating. The money I have in the house is losing its value every year. But I can't afford buying and selling costs, bigger monthly payments, and a higher interest rate. I'm thankful I can meet my present payments. My six-year-old car sputters and misses. When it finally stops, I don't know what I'll do."

"When my husband walked out on me, he left me hundreds of dollars on our credit cards to pay for," another divorcee said. "I sold our house and moved into a small apartment."

"It's been medical bills for me," a widow said. "My husband's lingering illness totalled over $10,000." Usually widows receive help from the husband's estate such as insurance policies, pensions, Social Security benefits, and family savings. In some cases such ample provision has been made that the family is cared for comfortably. But in other cases the drop in the standard of living is like the swift descent of an elevator in a 20-story building.

Even then the financial situation of widows is usually more stable and certain than the income of divorcees. Although the law states that child support should be provided for children until they are 18, recent statistics show that 90 percent default in their payments. "A divorcee can consider herself lucky if she gets financial help for two years," a lawyer said. "Most marriages that break up have experienced financial difficulties prior to the legal divorce. Having two households to support later only complicates the situation."

The result is that most widows and divorcees with families go job hunting. Many have had little or no training. Others have not worked for so many years that their skills are rusty. If they are professional people, they may find themselves almost

hopelessly behind the times. A middle-aged nurse, taking a con-
centrated course to update her on medical techniques, held in
her hand a two-inch thick blue blook. "These are the drugs I
have to become familiar with," she said. "Ninety percent of
them have been discovered since I first nursed."

In situations where women find their training lagging, the
median income for them often is little more than half of the income for single-parent families headed by white men. For black
women it is even worse.

The single biggest expense next to house payments and
food often is care for children. Added to this is the difficulty of
finding good day-care centers, although both the federal
government and churches are seeking ways to assist these
working women by establishing more good day care centers
and by subsidizing the cost.

Divorcees and widows also are often considered poor risks
and find it difficult to get credit. "I just keep on using my husband's credit cards," one widow said.

Some women manage everyday expenses, but emergencies produce near panic. One mother said, "When an appliance
breaks down or I see paint peeling off the house, I get a hollow,
sick feeling in my middle. I just can't afford to hire someone to
do my work, and I'm limited, both in my skills and in my time."
Financial worries aren't the only concerns.

*Concern for Children.* Some authorities link the rising
divorce rate with the sharp increases of juvenile court cases. At
least one judge, however, wasn't sure this assessment was correct. "Maybe," he said, "but I wonder if we don't have almost as
many cases from homes where husband and wife continue to
live together but fight all the time. And thousands of
youngsters survive divorce or death of a parent very well."

If the children do not get involved in juvenile court, other
troublesome problems often rear their heads: anxiety, guilt, insecurity, resentment, hostility, withdrawal, silent suffering and
jealousy.

In divorce cases, visits by the absent parent can cause further eruptions. Children often are caught in the bind of how to

show affection for one parent without betraying the other. Neighbors sometimes in the beginning become hypercritical of children in a home just split by divorce and tend to boss the children.

*Social Life.* Finding ways to meet people socially is another problem.

"I long so for social life, and especially to be able to talk with a man," another woman said. "Goodness knows, there's precious little time in the week left over for me, but even if I find a couple of hours, where will I go?"

"The church is for families," the widow of a pastor declared, after a year of trying to fit into her church in the new role as a single. "The Sunday morning service is for all, but beyond that?"

"I know," said another widow. "At our last congregational supper I was ushered to a table with a few other singles, way in the back of the room. It would have been much more enjoyable sitting with the couples."

One widow shared how she was trying to solve that problem. Once or twice a month she gives a dinner party to which she invites two couples and two single people. "We have a wonderful time," she said, "and some invite me back in turn. But even if they don't, it gives me an opportunity for male companionship without causing jealousy on the part of the wife, because I make it a point to invite different couples all the time." She smiled a bit ruefully. "But it's almost impossible, I've discovered, for a widow or divorcee to have a single close male friend. We have to find our close friendships with women."

*Loneliness.* But perhaps the most difficult of all problems is the never-ceasing loneliness.

After her divorce a woman fled to a large city to begin a new life. She took a room on the fourth floor of the YWCA where other divorced women were staying, and where it was quiet. "The walls were paper-thin," she said. "That first night I lay in bed and listened to a woman in the other room cry for two hours."

"I don't know what I'd do without my work," one new

widow said. "But the hardest part of the day is coming home to an empty house."

"It's not just having someone with whom you can talk over problems," another said. "If the children are on their own and managing fine, as mine are, there aren't problems to face every day. But it's just not having someone with whom you can share all the happenings of the day—the small talk."

"And there's the restless longing inside for a mate," another confessed. "Someone you love and give yourself to totally: emotionally, physically, intellectually. The old search is on again. I find myself looking, wondering . . . "

"I know," said another, "and I tell myself to be realistic and remember there are far more women over 40 than there are available men. But I still keep looking."

## Learning to Cope

In spite of their problems, most widowed and divorced singles do learn to cope.

Mary's husband died when she was only 50. Mary was a registered nurse but hadn't worked for 25 years. But with a son to help through medical school Mary decided to go back to college to receive the training that would enable her to get a good job. She lived in a dorm and worked as head resident which provided a little extra income for her. Mary earned a degree in speech and hearing therapy, then went on to get her master's degree. "Sometimes the going was rough," her daughter admitted, "but she completed her studies, and we are very proud of her."

Sharon's husband walked out on her, leaving her with three children to support. She began selling cosmetics, then took courses in developing poise and good grooming. Today her schedule is full as she gives lectures in public schools, to girl scouts, airline stewardesses, and sales clerks in department stores.

Life lost meaning for Ruth when both her husband and only child were killed. Stunned, she could do nothing for months. Finally volunteer work among developmentally handicapped children brought balm and healing. As her love for them grew, she determined to give the rest of her life for them. She enrolled in college taking special courses to help the developmentally handicapped, received her degree, and taught several years before her retirement.

Another woman, divorced with one child to care for, found self-pity draining away when she accepted an opportunity to serve.

"I commuted every night to a farm twenty miles away," she recounts. "There in the kitchen of an extremely rundown shack I taught English to two refugee couples and learned the most significant lesson of my life.

"These people had experienced communist terrorism, the loss of property and wealth, the death of loved ones. They had children die in their arms. They had experienced hunger, disease and any other form of privation you might care to name. They understood life at its primary level, and they accepted it accordingly.

"Even though I taught sometimes with my coat and boots on, huddled in front of the one faulty gas heater that once tried to gas us, I went in every night with a grateful heart for the serenity and love that was expressed in the homes of these refugees.

"They were thankful to be in our country, to be alive, and to be together. Somehow my problems came to feel plastic, self-imposed and a foolish extravagance. I didn't need them. They could be disregarded. I realize now how easy it is to worry over things in our society that are really not all that significant . . . I now teach a college course called English as a Second Language full-time and am dedicated to the future of this program."

**Those Who Have Never Married**

The situation of those who have never married is unique in some respects. The person who has never married is looked at askance. Society continues to insist marriage is the norm, though even statistically speaking, if monogamy is followed, marriage for all is impossible. Perhaps no one realizes this more clearly than the unmarried Christian woman.

Why is she unmarried? Some choose to remain single: to care for aging parents or a handicapped relative, to pursue advance study or a career that is either very demanding or calls for mobility. A few just enjoy the freedom of being single and don't want the responsibilities of marriage. A handful do not like children. But perhaps most are single simply because they do not meet someone whom they can love and who loves them in return.

*Emotional and Financial Problems.* The person who has never married may face unique emotional problems. As one expressed it: "During the middle years one begins, not only to face up to the fact that she is not married, but one also begins to find the reasons, in some cases, why she is not. This discovery is even more disturbing. Pride, self-protection, fears, invulnerability, among other things, have stood in the way, and I realize now that things might have been different."

Even with income tax hitting him hard, the single man usually is better off financially than his counterpart. One reason for this, in some cases, may be that, as studies have shown, single women often do not invest their savings in ways that could bring sizable returns. They seem afraid to take risks. Thus when they arrive at the middle years, and retirement becomes imminent, they often become concerned as to whether or not they will have enough to care for themselves.

"Some mornings I wake up with a tight tension band around my head," the secretary to a vice president of a corporation said. Her employer had just retired. The man who had moved up to replace him brought with him his own secretary. The company was at a loss to know what to do with the secretary who had worked for them for over 25 years. "I go to work and stare at my face reflected in the polish of an empty desk," the secretary said. "They keep telling me there will be something for me. But will there? And what will it be? Will I be dropped to the basement? Farmed out? Invited to retire early? Will they decide the retirement benefits I have accrued are going to be too costly for the company so they'll give me work so demeaning I'll resign of my own volition? I wonder about all this, and the band around my head gets tighter and tighter."

*Difficulty in Achieving Independence.* The single man who continues to live at home might discover after a while that he is not allowed to grow up. Although he may have younger brothers and sisters who are completely free, he may be treated like a child. One single complained his mother still tells him when to shampoo his hair, what shirt to wear, and even asks what time he will be home at night.

The woman who continues to live at home often does not realize all the implications at first. Her job absorbs her interest. She is content to have her own room and luxuriates in having all her needs cared for: house cleaned, meals cooked, laundry done. Often not until she has reached her middle years does discontent set in. Then she begins to wish she had a little home of her own or even an apartment where she could come and go at will and furnished as she would like. A friend tells her: "I come home from work dead tired. Often I lie down and sleep until 8:00 P.M.. Then I awaken refreshed and prepare myself a good dinner and really enjoy my evening." The one at home, still fenced in by parents' routine feels envious. Resentment begins to smoulder. Tension builds up.

But would it be fair, at this point, to ask the aging parents to adapt their way of life to hers? They have, after all, spent 20 or 30 years adjusting their lives, seeking the welfare of their children, although this is difficult for anyone who is not a parent to understand. Can a child take and take from parents for years and years with little responsibility then not extend that same care to the parents later in life when they need it?

*Resentments Which May Develop.* The tension which develops can become a wall, not only between the adult child and the aging parents but also between the single adult and God, preventing the person from receiving the help God stands ready to give.

Even singles living on their own may experience resentment toward God—resentment because of having to carry life's load alone, or having to face the insecurity of retirement alone, of lying ill alone in their apartments, of not having normal sexual drives satisfied, of being *the* child expected to care for the aging parents.

The single may be tempted to feel she is not desirable or wanted (I say *she* simply because more women than men face the problem.) This, in turn, can produce inferiority feelings of worthlessness, of not liking or being able to accept one's self. Self-pity is at hand to smother one. It is only a step from there to bitterness, sarcasm, and a critical spirit. Having no one to whom it is necessary to defer or consider, it becomes all too easy to become egocentric, thinking mainly of one's self, spending one's money on elaborate wardrobes or costly vacations— or hoarding it with vigilance. Rigidity can set in also so the slightest interruption of one's schedule can prove upsetting or the expression of another's point of view cannot be tolerated.

But there is a way out. First, the inner resentment toward God should be surrendered. One then seeks grace to accept the present situation and thank God for it. This calls for *faith*, because we cannot see all the factors God can. We have to believe he knows best.

We might have to make this declaration of faith and surrender over and over. It is difficult to be so decisive that temptations never come again, but following the initial surrender, subsequent relinquishments of our hold on our "rights" should be easier.

When our resentment has been brought to Christ, who will cleanse us from it, we can proceed.

We recognize we are not unique in having problems. Even married people do. It is helpful to sit down and list all we have going for us. All of us need to accept the fact that we may have to live with a certain amount of loneliness. But if we are single, we are free in ways married people are not. We can explore avenues of service open to us because we are single and mobile; we can be adventuresome and choose almost any career we wish.

Developing a positive, thankful attitude helps. Finding a substitute family enriches our lives. Even our avocations can be turned outward to benefit others. We can cultivate new friends, of different social status and race and backgrounds, and as we do, in a few instances, we might even find a mate. For nothing attracts another as much as a person who is vibrantly alive and happy. Not that finding a mate need be the goal necessarily. Single life can be complete and intensely rewarding and interesting.

### Living a Rewarding Life

We all know singles who have transformed small houses or apartments into attractive homes reflecting the personality of the person living there, singles who unselfishly have shared their lives with their extended families and become favorite aunts and uncles, singles who live rich, purposeful and satisfying lives. Many pastors can testify to dedicated, faithful service given by the singles within the congregation. And what would have happened to the advance and growth of Christ's church overseas without all the single missionaries? Sometimes, while serving overseas we used to say jokingly, "The woman is the man to do the job!" One wonders sometimes if the lives of these singles would have been as fruitful if marriage had placed its restraints on them?

I think, for example, of Marion Gould of St. Paul, Minnesota. When she was in her teens it seemed to her that the world was passing her by. Severe acne masked the attractiveness of her bright, pleasant face and isolated her from friends and fun. Marion watched friends date and become engaged and listened to their plans for marriage.

Never mind, Marion thought, I'll be a career woman. Both the education and medical fields appealed to her. She was a brilliant student and won a scholarship to a college in her home town. But these were depression years, and Marion's parents just didn't have the money needed for Marion to attend college.

"Never mind," Marion comforted her father, "you have given me a prize far greater than any education. You have helped me know God."

"He'll never let you down either," her father said, "only" —referring to her education—"I wish it could have been different." He thought for a while, then added, "Why don't we pray you will find work? Then you can save your money and go to college?"

But it was not to be. Marion's father became ill with terminal cancer. After two pain-filled years he died, leaving Marion with staggering medical bills to pay and an ailing mother to care for.

Marion enjoyed the work she was doing in an office, but she kept praying, "Lord, surely there must be more to life than just earning a living. Surely you must have some plan for me, something that will have purpose and meaning."

A door opened. Her pastor wished that the children of their church could worship on a level that would be more meaningful to them. Would Marion be willing to assume responsibility for a children's church on Sunday mornings? Yes, Marion said.

"It called for a lot of imagination and hard work," Marion admitted. "There were no set programs or lesson plans, but I saw it as a wonderful opportunity to get close to the children and to win them to Christ and lead them into fields of service for him."

Marion understood that "getting close" meant playing with the children too, so she planned picnics, Halloween parties, Christmas parties, and outings. Every Sunday morning she arose early to pick up underprivileged children who had no other way of getting to church.

God touched the hearts of the children. They began to respond. The work was rewarding, but still Marion was not satisfied. "You must have something else for me to do, Lord," she prayed. "I can do more. Besides, I should be pointing the children to interests beyond themselves."

A friend suggested she investigate the work of a mission in India. Marion sat down to write a letter.

At the same time, at the mission in India, two little Brahmin girls arrived. Both their parents had died. The little girls were considered witches and had been cast out. A former orphan of the mission found the starving, frightened children and brought them to the mission. Sherada (Wisdom) was six, Seroj (Lotus) was four.

When one of the women at the mission received Marion's letter of inquiry she wrote asking if Marion would like to support Seroj. Thus began a mother-daughter relationship that was to continue for more than 20 years.

Marion, not only sent monthly support checks for Seroj, but she loved her as her own. She remembered her with gifts at Christmas, her birthday, and special days. She sent weekly letters. In time Seroj could write English and she began to answer Marion's letters directly. Marion prayed for Seroj always.

She began to see her prayers answered. When Seroj was in the fifth grade she said she believed in Christ and wanted to be baptized. When she graduated from high school she said she wanted to train for service. Nursing was open so she enrolled.

"At first," Seroj confessed to Marion, "I could hardly stand the smells and sights and wondered why I had ever chosen this training. Besides, the studies and work were hard, and I felt rebellious. But I love God's Word, and as I have been turning to it I have been able to draw the strength needed to carry on."

Seroj was able to complete the first year with success. The next year was better. Her final year of training, however, was exceptionally difficult, and she would get so discouraged and tired she was tempted to quit. But she hung in.

A number of young men approached Seroj, but her heart was set on a young doctor who showed her attention and affection. But Seroj had misinterpreted his attentions. When he made it clear he was not thinking of marriage there were tears, heartache, and disappointment.

"She was wanting to make her own choice," Marion said. "I wrote her, counselling her to seek God's will and reminding her that:

> God knows, he loves, he cares.
> Nothing this truth can dim.
> He gives the very best to those
> Who leave the choice with him."

God did have other plans. As Seroj began to pray a Christian family in another part of India was also seeking God's guidance in regard to the right girl for their youngest son to marry.

Seroj herself tells the story:

"Their son, Suresh, was far away in America, studying in a seminary. But he returned to India for a visit and was told then that his father's health was not good. His family advised him to find a Christian girl so his father would have the joy of meeting her. So the family began the search. They had a list of 37 names. Unknown to me, my name was one of the 37. Suresh's family had heard about me and knew that I was a nurse serving God here in the Mukti hospital. They were told that I loved the Lord and wanted to serve him. So Suresh and his older brother traveled to Mukti to inquire about me.

"Suresh and I met . . . and it was love at first sight! Suresh and I talked and talked, and he explained to me how he was studying in America to become a pastor. My heart leaped with joy and praise to God!

"We both agreed to spend much time in prayer to know God's will. Prayer only deepened the assurance that God meant us for each other. I marvelled at God's plans for me. I never would have dreamed that I would have the opportunity of visiting America and meeting those who have loved and prayed for me through the years. God truly showed me that if we are faithful in leaving the choice with him, he will always give us his very best."

Seroj came to America to be united with her husband who had returned there to continue his seminary studies. After 20 years Marion met the daughter she had loved and for whom she had prayed. A year later Marion became grandmother when a little boy was born to Seroj and Suresh Borde. And then Marion waved them off as they flew back to India to begin their work.

In the meantime, during the years Seroj was in high school Marion had told an American missionary in Korea about the work of the mission in India. He incorporated some of the procedures and policies that had worked well for the older experienced India mission in the Compassionate Orphanage he was founding, and he was grateful to Marion for her help.

Seroj was launched in life. The Compassionate Orphanage

in Korea was engaged in a ministry of caring. The objective Marion had set for herself in the children's church was being realized; over 200 children had committed themselves to Christ. Her position as one of the secretaries of a large corporation was challenging and satisfying. Her salary was enough to share with children of nieces and nephews and to help support many missionaries. And still Marion was not satisfied.

So she "adopted" Yung Ae (which means Lovely Child), a homeless Korean waif about whom no one knew anything and began to love and support and pray for her as she had for Seroj. Eventually Yung Ae took training at a trade school which gave her the sewing skills she needed to earn her own living.

Retirement was drawing closer for Marion. "But surely, Lord," she prayed, "there is yet one other I can love for you." And so she accepted Saraswati, a 12-year-old Indian girl whose mother had lived with a man in a common-law marriage. When both parents died Saraswati was left to care for her eight-year-old brother and six-year-old sister. All the children were starving when someone brought them to the mission.

Reflecting on her life Marion says simply, "My life could have been a barren and defeated one, but what glorious joy there has been for me in experiencing the fulfillment of God's purposes. 'Oh, the depth of the riches of the wisdom and knowledge of God! How unsearchable are his judgments and his ways past finding out!'"

**How the Church Can Help**

What can churches do to stretch out a hand of friendship to the singles to draw them into the circle of the congregational family from which they often feel they are outcasts?

Large churches have and are activating special programs for singles. Some single groups come together on Sunday mornings to share in Bible study and spiritual inspiration. After church they may go to a local restaurant for lunch. Other groups may meet during the week to discuss everyday problems, beliefs, joys, and troublesome feelings. Frequently, on Saturday nights some single groups will get together for potlucks, theater parties, or various other recreational activities.

Some single groups have organized "help committees" with a chairperson who steers those with the know-how to homes plagued with leaky faucets or plugged drains. Other churches encourage singles to become actively involved in some area of service in the church. In one church a Youth Partners program, patterned after the Big Brother program, provides a father or mother figure for the child deprived of one or the other.

In the end, however, the needs of the singles are best met on a spiritual basis. Introducing them to Jesus Christ and nourishing their Christian faith is the most significant contribution any church can make. This is the distinctive role of the church. The church must keep all of its groups redemptive. The group must not become just another club.

Small churches usually find they can minister best by initiating joint programs with other local churches. A few singles resent any "singling out." "I belong to a small church," one said. "I'm happy there. I count. I'm accepted. I'm not considered odd, but just one of them." This, undoubtedly, is the ideal.

Many family counselors have expressed the wish that more families would include singles in their family circle. "It calls for a rare married woman to do so," one divorcee said almost bitterly. "My experience has been that soon after I become friends with a couple, the woman begins to eye me with suspicion. I represent a threat."

Singles, as well as married people, need to pause midway in life to consider their goals, examine them to see if they are worthy, and then set for themselves reasonable goals. Working toward definite goals can be one of the best substitutes for sex, and it trims loneliness to a tolerable level.

Hopefully, this chapter also has pulled back the curtain a little and let married people look in briefly on what life is like for a single person. All too often we walk around with stereotyped mental pictures that are incorrect. Perhaps as we married people set new goals for the second halves of our lives one of our goals can be to learn how to love and include some singles in our lives. For eventually the day will come for us who are married now when we too will be single.

## For Thought and Reflection

All of us have some basic heart hungers. Note those to which you feel you need to give some attention, hungers that you feel are not being adequately satisfied or fulfilled.

*I feel accepted. I have some unit to which I belong. (Name it).*

*I am giving love to others and helping to meet the needs of others. (Who are they?)*

*I feel valued, recognized and affirmed by others. (By whom?)*

*I have adequate intellectual, recreational, aesthetic and spiritual growth opportunities. (What are they?)*

*I have a few people who I know care deeply for me, who are warm in showing affection and on whom I know I can depend. (Who are they?)*

*I have certain, definite responsibilities. (What are they?)*

*I think I am realistic in accepting reality. (In what respects?)*

*I respect the rights of others. (Who are your "others"?)*

*I enjoy the freedom I have. (To do what?)*

*I respect differences. (Between you and who else?)*

*I have learned to distance myself. (From what?)*

*I have faith in God. (As evidenced by . . . )*

*I have trust in God. (As evidenced by . . . )*

*The values that are dear to me are:* (These are reflected in my
  life by: . . . )

Look carefully at the points you checked. Now write down
what you can do to increase fulfillment of these basic needs of
the heart.

# 9

# Will We Have Enough Stored Up for Winter?

> *Final security is a matter of faith. It is what we believe about ourselves, others, about the purpose of life, and about God that determines our deepest security.*
> —Lowell Russell Ditzen

Ask six of your friends what their chief concerns are midstream in life and all six will put security near the top of the list. But chances are they will also mention the need to do something different, in order to get rid of the "blahs" in their life. At the same time, while they might not refer to it, the burden of assuming responsibility for a million different things actually is consuming most of their time.

Are these three needs: the need for security, the need for adventure, and the need for assuming responsibility, actually opposed to each other? Not really. In fact, handled properly they can fit together like pieces of a puzzle.

True, our need for adventure may be stifled because of our fear of taking risks. But understanding where true security lies actually will enable us to take risks. Adventure becomes most satisfying when it is linked with our need to assume responsibility. The following three chapters form a trilogy. They are closely related to each other, and each is concerned with how we can satisfy in meaningful and valid ways three of our basic needs: the need for security, adventure, and assuming responsibility.

It is important that we satisfy these needs aright. Unmet needs give birth to frustration, dissatisfaction, irritability, and complaining and can prevent us from growing and developing as persons.

Let's think, first of all, of the need for security. How do we attempt to answer our need for security? To what do we turn?

## Loyal Mates

We all want the security that comes with knowing our mate loves us. A young man in one of the college classes I attended told me one day: "My father and mother were separated for a while. Now they are together again, but Dad is so afraid he'll do something to upset Mom he's all tied up in knots. He told me last night the tension was getting almost unbearable, and he didn't know how much longer he could stand it."

That husband is not secure in his relationship with his wife. How different the words of George Eliot in "The Essence of Friendship": "Oh, the comfort, the inexpressible comfort of feeling safe with a person, having neither to weigh nor measure words, but to pour them all out, just as they are, chaff and grain together, knowing that a faithful hand will take and sift them, keep what is worth keeping, and then, with the breath of kindness blow the rest away."

Many read that wistfully and wish that were true of their married life. With steadily rising divorce rates, some wonder uneasily if it will happen to them next.

## Friends and Self-Esteem

Knowing we have loved ones, relatives and friends, to whom we can turn at a time of need does bring a sense of security. We can face almost anything if we know we won't have to face it alone.

But even good friends might forsake us. There is as much treason in the world as friendship. The disciples left Jesus and fled. It is very unlikely we shall be able to go through life without being betrayed by some friends. While we do well to cultivate and nourish friendships, still our ultimate hope for security cannot rest with our friends.

Some of us might still be seeking the security that comes from an assurance of self-worth. When my husband was a pastor in Canada, he was called upon to officiate at the funeral of a man who had lived a hermit existence in a shack in the back woods. There was no one to mourn his death, absolutely no one, so completely had he lived apart from people.

Why had this man withdrawn from society? His secret remains locked within him. We can only speculate. Was he so unsure of himself and so fearful of what lay out in the world that his only security was in withdrawal? How different it could have been if he had been able to see himself as a person created and loved by God and therefore as a person of infinite worth. This would have made him strong and enabled him to take his place in the world as a contributing member. Happy that person who develops self-assurance early in life, but, thank God, it never is too late.

Even when we have developed a healthy sense of self-esteem things can happen to us in life that eat away at it. Children might do things that we feel tarnish the family name. We may not be able to succeed in our ventures to the degree we had hoped. Our marriage might crumble. Any number of things might happen that cause us to doubt our worth. Our security cannot rest in a strong sense of self-esteem, important as it is.

Developing and perfecting new skills is one way to cultivate self-confidence. A man who had experienced periodic spells of being laid off from work approached me on the church patio one Sunday morning with a beaming face.

"Brighter days should be ahead for us," he said. "Wife and I talked over our situation. We thought about what each of us enjoyed doing most and do best. We asked ourselves if job opportunities in those fields were plentiful right across the nation. After investigation we decided they were. So we took time out and both of us got some specialized training. Now we're both working, both enjoying our work and both reasonably sure we shall be able to get a job wherever we go. It's a good feeling."

Their decision had been wise, but to put all one's trust in one's own cleverness or ability is hardly safe. A few months later this man's wife became ill with a lingering, baffling disease. The family lost half their source of income and even with the help of medical insurance, bills mounted. Once again this family felt acutely the need for financial security.

## Financial Security

The person in the middle years is very aware of the need for financial security. A major problem, however, is that although people know they should save both for post-retirement needs and emergencies, what with mortgage payments, orthodontist bills, college tuition, and the ever-rising cost of living one never seems able to save—at least not as much as they would like. To cheer themselves up, they rationalize that they should have at least ten good earning years after the children are on their own, when it should be possible to save. Aren't life insurance policies, real estate, and pension plans a form of savings? And yet they wish more could be saved.

We need the security that comes with knowing how to care for the financial affairs of our family. Wives and husbands should be equally knowledgeable.

The husband of a friend of mine dropped dead at work one day. He had cared for all the business transactions of the family. His widow didn't know even how to write a check. Her confusion added to her already troubled state of mind. "If only," she lamented, "we had taken time to sit down and get all the information together in one book in a way I could understand." Many insurance companies have booklets where financial information can be entered in an orderly fashion.

Even at middle age some couples are having problems living within their budgets. If this is a problem for you, here are some questions to consider:

1. Are we spending too much on housing?
2. Do we have too many cars or too-expensive-to-operate cars?

3. Do we feel compelled to keep up with others?
4. Does either of our generous expense accounts at work make us tend to overspend at home?
5. Do our hobbies cost more than fits our budget?
6. Are we spending too much on clothes? Should we be wearing our clothes longer?
7. Are we spending too much on our children? Is it necessary that their clothes are the latest, popular fashion?
8. Are we impulse buyers?
9. Do we buy depreciable items on credit?
10. Do we pay our bills promptly?
11. Do we keep careful record so we know exactly where our money is going?
12. Do we tithe?

There are other questions to consider if we are going to enjoy a feeling of security in regard to finances: Have we made adequate provision for our family in case of death? Have we made wills? If so, are they up-to-date? Stationery and book stores also sell financial planning books in which we can enter all the information our family should have if either of us dies. Have we a record like this? *Are* both husband and wife knowledgeable in regard to financial affairs? Does our family know our wishes in regard to funeral and burial arrangements? Do we take reasonable precautions in regard to safeguarding our home against burglary and fire? Do we have lists of our furnishings or pictures of the rooms of our home?

Even those who plan carefully and think everything is in order sometimes worry. What if another depression, such as that of the 1930s, strikes? What guarantee is there that there will be Social Security benefits by the time we retire? If housing costs continue to escalate and inflation isn't curbed, how can we be sure that the income we have after retirement will be adequate?

From a practical point of view, if any of these things should happen we probably will discover how many corners we can cut and how many things there are that we can get along without—nicely.

From a spiritual point of view times of need can become occasions of learning to trust God in new ways. It's better than worrying and, in the end, less expensive because it just might keep us out of the hospital.

## True Security

What *does* make us feel secure? A loyal spouse? Trusted friends? Health? A steady job? A pocket full of skills from which we can draw? A stable government? A reliable law enforcement system? Insurance policies? Justice in the courts? Hospitalization insurance? Retirement funds? Savings?

But what if all these should crumble? It happened to Job. It has happened to others since. It happened to Ann.

Ann had grown up in a Christian home. She married and three children gladdened their home. Even the usually troubled years of adolescence seemed flowing quite smoothly. Relieved of some of her home responsibilities Ann enrolled in a weekly Bible class.

"Then it was that I really started to put things together as far as my Christian faith was concerned," Ann said. "My walk with the Lord became serious, and I began to put into practice what I was learning. Little did I realize then that the Lord was preparing me for what lay ahead. For the last six years have been as close to a nightmare as I ever want to experience."

It began one evening when Ann went to answer the doorbell and found police officers standing outside.

"We have custody of your son Peter," they said after a few questions to verify that they were at the right house.

"You have what?" Ann almost shouted.

The charges of rape seemed unbelievable. Peter was only seventeen. Only later did Ann learn of his close association with a homosexual neighbor, an older man, who delighted in showing Peter pornographic pictures, instructing him and molesting him, trying to convince Peter that he too was a homosexual. Dismayed and confused Peter had reacted by trying to prove he was heterosexual, not homosexual, by raping the woman.

Peter's case dragged on and on, interminably. Lawyers had to be hired. Expenses mounted at an alarming rate. However, Peter was fortunate to qualify for therapy. "He's not the typical rapist," the judge said. "We must do all we can to help him."

Still, visiting their son in jail was a shattering experience for Ann and her husband, Mike. Later Peter was transferred to a hospital far enough away so it was difficult to visit him even weekly.

Ann's husband, Mike, had his own business. The business began to show signs of the stress Mike was feeling. The rest of the family felt it too. Peter's older married sister, Madeline, began to quarrel with her husband. Peter's older brother, Eric, took his frustration, anger and anxiety out on his young wife. Madeline's marriage wavered and tottered, then straightened itself and survived. Not so Eric's. His young wife wearied of Eric's bad temper, and one day walked out on him, taking their child with her.

Finally, after what seemed an eternity, Peter was released. He was still required to report regularly. Getting employment proved difficult also, and, in fact, he was told it would never be easy for him.

Then Mike had to undergo heart bypass surgery. When he came home from the hospital he would not allow himself time to recuperate but plunged into work. There were bills and more bills to pay. He bought additional equipment and hired more workers. At the same time he bagan to act strangely. He forgot things. He mislaid important documents. And he became, not only fiercely self-defensive, but aggressive and even ugly.

Dismayed and confused, Ann didn't know what to do. She had been doing the office work for the business in their home, but Mike became so explosive and impossible to work for that finally she asked him to hire another secretary/bookkeeper. To gain a little respite and find relief for a few hours each day Ann took a job away from home.

Then it was that Eric, stopping by at his parent's home one mid-morning found his dad had blown his head off.

Eric then took over his father's business. For six months things seemed to go well, but lack of experience and his youthfulness tripped up Eric, and the business was forced to go into bankruptcy. Feeling totally unable to cope, Eric ran away. For days Ann did not know where he was or what had happened to him. He finally sent her word, but stayed away for months.

Ann then gladly accepted the offer of one of the older men who had been working for them to manage the business on a partnership basis. A few months later though, because of personality problems she had to terminate this arrangement.

Peter, in the meantime, had found a church home, was growing in his faith, and in addition to his regular job had taken an early morning newspaper delivery job. One morning he tapped a young jogger on her shoulder and asked her the time. She screamed, "Rape!" and ran to the security guard of the apartment complex. Peter's old record condemned him, and he was sent off again for treatment.

Eric arrived home only to announce that he was hooked on both alcohol and drugs and asked his mother for $2,000 for a rehab program. Ann dug into her already depleted savings.

The business had folded. Ann found a job, but after a few months the company went bankrupt. Her dishwasher conked out. It seemed there was to be no end to trouble.

It was at this point that Ann gave her testimony one evening in her church.

"I have suffered much," she said. "There's been endless, awful pain. Through it all I've been able to continue my walk with the Lord because time and again he has picked me up and carried me. This really and truly can happen if you let go and let God.

"At first it was difficult to put my problems in Jesus' hands and leave them there. I would take them back and try to work out things myself. Over and over I did this.

"Then little by little, through hard-core, gutsy perseverance, I began to persistently and doggedly apply what I had heard. In obedience to God I would admit my fear and state my problem. Then I would deliberately commit it to him and dump all the pressure on him and stubbornly refuse to take it back. As I continued resolutely to do this, I experienced Jesus Christ acting on my behalf. No matter how deeply I was hurting or how much I felt misunderstood or how achingly I wanted to quit, he was there. Every time I began to reel as I felt the bottom dropping out Christ stepped in and steadied me.

"The Lord provides things money cannot buy. With him I have experienced testing such as I had never imagined. In the midst of it all I have discovered true security. Christ has given me purpose for living, a renewed sense of direction, a deep peace, understanding, a compassionate heart and a wisdom I had never experienced before. As I rest in him his character traits are being formed in me. All these are priceless gifts of the spirit which no one can ever take away from me. This does not mean I no longer make mistakes. I still do, lots of them—dumb ones! But thank the Lord, his forgiveness is instantly available. And I feel secure in him."

The dictionary defines security as "safety, protection, freedom from uncertainty or doubt." But it also defines it as "the condition of being firmly fastened or secured." Those who are fastened to the Lord, who cling to him, are secure. They know God will meet their needs whatever those needs are.

"My savings have shrunk, and my monthly income is small," an 84-year-old woman told me. "But the Lord looks after me. Two years ago I felt prompted to increase my hospitalization insurance. I didn't know at the time that the next two years would bring heavy medical expenses. I went blind for a while. The doctor thought I would never see again. But I don't have resources to pay someone to care for all my needs. So I prayed, and the Lord restored enough vision so I can take care of myself. I needed a new coat and shoes, and my watch had broken. On my birthday I received some cash gifts. I went down to a department store and found both the coat and shoes on sale and had enough left to buy a watch. So, you see," she said contentedly, "the Lord takes care of his own. It's like the

Psalmist said, 'I have been young and now am old, but I have not seen God's people begging bread.'"

The serene faith and trust of this old saint reflects the spirit Jesus wanted to see in his followers when he said, "Be not anxious." In today's language Jesus probably would say, "Don't come apart, don't go to pieces," Those who are secure in God may seem to come apart and go to pieces for a time, but as they turn to God, he picks up the pieces and puts them together again. God has promised to care for us. This certainty can strengthen and reassure us, weak and confused though we may feel. It is this assurance, this conviction, that we need most.

A Minnesota farmer, father of five, awakened one night with severe pain in his shoulder. Within 24 hours his right arm dangled useless at his side. Several weeks later the doctors at Mayo Clinic diagnosed his trouble as acute bilateral brachial plexitis, a rare nerve disease. The doctors were dubious as to whether he would ever regain the use of his arms.

"The day they broke that news to us it was gray and raining," his wife said. "We walked back to our motel room. I picked up my Bible, and a tract tumbled out. I read these words of F. B. Meyer: 'Never act in panic . . . wait upon God until he makes known his way. He accounts himself responsible for all the results of keeping thee where thou art.'

"If God is willing to assume responsibility for what has happened to us, we can trust him," the wife said. They committed themselves to God.

Olaf, her husband commented many months later after he had regained the use of his right arm and partial use of his left one: "I think the fact I was a farmer made it easier for me to accept in an attitude of trust what had happened to me. Rain—too much or too little—storms, sickness in the herd, blight, pests, hail—all have taught me to accept disappointments, failures, illnesses, and setbacks and carry on patiently. All of these I have learned to consider only as opportunities to grow in faith and trust in God. Thus during my illness, though at times I felt frustrated, I never felt licked. We never doubted that God would see us through." He paused for a moment. "That doesn't mean it was easy," he added.

Stella, his wife interjected, "I remember the day the trucks came and hauled away the cows. Olaf wept."

"I remember days you cried too," Olaf countered.

Both laughed. "But those days were infrequent," Olaf said. "We kept reminding each other of the lines of that old hymn: 'His love in times past, forbids me to think, he'll leave me at last in trouble to sink.'"

For the Christian, security does not mean being shielded or saved from danger, risk or evil. Rather it means knowing God is with us, regardless of what comes. "In the world you *will have* tribulation," Jesus assured his followers, but then he quickly added, "but be of good cheer! I have overcome the world." Jesus is with us. This assurance will see us through.

The ability of humans to survive almost unbelievable tragedy and danger if they feel secure in the presence of trusted others was illustrated during World War II in Britain. The cities were being bombed. Hundreds of the children were sent to homes in the country where they could be cared for and be safe. A few parents, however, chose to keep their children with them. Surprisingly enough, the children who had their parents with them, though they were exposed to danger, survived better than those who lived in safety, but separated from their parents.

If we are convinced God is with us and that he will never abandon us, we can know true security. With this security comes courage. With security and courage pooled up in our hearts we can face the future—any future—with confidence and calmness. We will find strength to be true to our convictions even when we are challenged and opposed. We will not hesitate to act when we are convinced that what we are doing is right. We can take necessary risks to respond to the call of duty.

"We are pressed on every side by trouble," Paul wrote to the Corinthian Christians, "but not crushed and broken. We are perplexed because we don't know why things happen as they do, but we don't give up and quit. We are hunted down, but God never abandons us. We get knocked down, but we get up again and keep going. These bodies of ours are constantly facing death just as Jesus did; so it is clear to all that it is only the living Christ within (who keeps us safe)." (2 Corinthians 4:8-10, Living Bible).

Thus secure in our God, as we assume the responsibilities we should in midlife, our need for adventure will be satisfied in the right way. It is this need we shall discuss next.

### For Study, Re-evaluation, and Discussion

1. What does the Bible say about friends? See: Proverbs 17:17; Proverbs 18; 24; Job 16:20; Job 19:14; Psalm 4:19; Psalm 55:12, 12; 38:11; Proverbs 19:6; Micah 7:5; Genesis 38:12; James 4:4; John 15:15; Proverbs 16:28; Job 42:10; Exodus 33:11; John 15:15; Hebrews 3:4; Job 29:1.

2. How strong is your support network? In the following exercise, circle one response for each item. Then add the scores next to each item you circled and put the total below.

1. At work, how many persons do you talk to about a job hassle? none (or not employed at present) (0); one or two (3); two or three (4); four or more (5). (This means, how many are there at your place of work in whom you feel you can confide, at least to a degree.)

2. How many neighbors do you trade favors with (loan tools or household items, share rides, babysitting, etc.)? none (0); one (1); two or three (2); four or more (3).

3. Do you have a spouse? no (0); you are married or are living with a friend or parent (10).

4. How often do friends and close family members visit you at home? rarely (0); about once a month (1); several times a month (4); once a week or more (8).

5. How many friends or family members do you talk to about personal matters? none (0); one or two (6); three to five (8); six or more (10).

6. How often do you participate in a social, community, sports or church group? rarely (0); about once a month (1); several times a month (2); once a week or more (4).

If your support network is less than 15, your network has

*low strength* and probably does not provide much support. You need to consider making more social contacts.

If your score is from 15 to 29, your network has *moderate strength* and likely will provide enough support except during periods of high stress.

If your score is 30 or more, your support network has *high strength,* and it will likely maintain you well even during periods of high tension.

3. How are we going to get support? Read:
   a. John 5:2-7.
   b. John 4:46 ff. John 4:7. Matthew 21:1-2, Matthew 26:17-19; Mark 14:32-42.
   c. Acts 16:15. Philippians 2:25; 4:14-16. Ruth 2:8-16.

4. Have there been times in your life when close friends have stepped meaningfully forward to give you the kind of help you needed? Have you been able to give this kind of help to any of your friends? Talk about this.

5. Overall, do you feel satisfied with your present financial situation?

6. If so, can you anticipate anything that might reverse that situation? Are you doing anything to be ready for such a contingency?

7. If you're not satisfied with your present financial situation, can you think of anything that might improve things? Are you doing anything about this?

8. Could you get along with less? What would your spouse think of you if you were to drastically reduce your spending? What would your children say? What would your neighbors or friends think or say? How would this affect you?

9. How does the way you spend your money tally with the priorities you have established for yourself and/or your family?

10. There is no single word in the English language that captures the full meaning of social support. But in the richness of the Spanish language, there is one word that does. That word is *confianza.* Ask a Spanish speaking friend to interpret the meaning of *confianza* for you.

11. How many instances in your life can you recall when God

enabled you to accept and bear something that otherwise would have been unbearable? Share this with your family or some friends.

12. What causes you anxiety? How can you deal with this anxiety? What have others in your group found helpful?

13. Harold Willis Dodds, one time president of Princeton University, stated once that concentration on security is not only suicidal for society as a whole, but it throttles the powers of the individual and starves his very soul. "Like happiness security at best is a by-product of the process of living," Dodds stated. "Courage is a better motto than security and offers far brighter prospects of social stability and self-reliance. The persons who keep their eyes fixed on security inevitably become enmeshed in the tentacles of the *status quo*. Engrossed in such a narrow objective they lose their best chance for security. Each of us requires the spur of insecurity to force us to do our best."

Consider also how far we as a nation have drifted into a philosophy of security where we view security as a condition where we are provided for materially in every respect. Originally we understood security as freedom, not *from* certain things, i.e. want, sickness, unemployment, etc., but rather freedom to *do* something: freedom to speak, to worship, to assemble, to work, to pursue happiness.

Discuss these differing viewpoints and how the one we adopt as our own will affect our own philosophy of security.

## 10

# Can I Learn to Ski and Skate at My Age?

*It is dangerous to have one's golden age behind one. It is the opposite of adventure. Life is a one-way street.*
—Paul Tournier

All of us, from time to time, get bored with our day to day and year to year routine and long for a new adventure. Persons in their middle years often feel the need acutely. They may have met it by advancing steadily in their jobs to this time, but now they have reached their peak. The adventure of advancement is dead. They find themselves still chained to their jobs. This is especially true for men who have been working for more years at their jobs than has been the case for their wives. Singles also often feel trapped in their jobs at an early age.

I'm afraid I'm a bit envious of my wife," one man said. "She went to work a few years ago when our children no longer needed all her attention. A whole new world opened to her. But myself . . . I just look forward to work and then more work, the same old work." He felt his days of adventure and exploration were behind him, and that the eight-to-five grind was all that remained for him.

It is important that we find right ways of satisfying our need for adventure, for if the need is not met, frustration and boredom set in. Then the drive for adventure can become so compelling it may lead us to satisfy it in wrong ways. This sometimes accounts for extra-marital affairs which are not un-common in middle age.

Becoming completely absorbed in outside activities is another way in which some seek to satisfy the need for adven-ture. Gaugin, at 45, abandoned a successful banking career and his family and went to Tahiti to paint.

During these days of liberating forces at work, some wives, enjoying their newly-found liberty when the children get older, become so caught up with and fascinated by their careers or the education they are pursuing that they neglect or turn their backs on family responsibilities and drift apart from their husbands. A few have even run away. When this is done another need is being overlooked: the need for assuming and continuing to bear responsibility.

Many seek satisfaction in second-hand ways. They lose themselves in adventure stories or science fiction or mysteries. They go to movies or watch TV, purely for escape.

Some time ago when I attended a ball game with our son I saw a middle-aged man become the self-appointed cheer leader for our section of spectators. Turning to face us, he gesticulated wildly, jumping up and down, causing the beer in the can he was grasping to fountain out and be spilled. He shouted to us to give all we had to cheers and boos. He was out to get adventure in a big way.

Others feverishly campaign for their political favorite, and after the election proudly proclaim, "*We* won!" Day-dreaming or fantasizing provide adventure for some persons or they rehearse their adventures of earlier years. Others wander from amusement park to amusement park. Braver ones venture out, and they themselves try soaring or roaring across fields in the winter in snowmobiles or shooting rapids in canoes. Have you ever noticed the number of older men zooming around in ex-pensive, high-powered, low-slung sports cars?

### Satisfying the Need for Adventure in Meaningful Ways

The need for adventure cries out for satisfaction whether or not people are aware of it. How can we satisfy it in meaningful and productive ways? *We can develop new skills.* There are many fields to explore.

Robert Frost had been farming in New Hampshire and teaching in prep schools. His restlessness grew until finally he sold all and went to England. There on his small farm he began to write poems. His first poem was published when he was 40.

Pearl Buck was just about 40 when her first novel *East Wind, West Wind* was published. She went on to win the Pulitzer Prize and the Nobel Prize writing in all almost 70 books.

George Bernard Shaw's literary career also began after he was 40.

Have you always wanted to write? Catherine Marshall used to suggest six characteristics of a writer:

1. Did you dream of writing when you were a child?
2. Do you love to write? Would you write without reward?
3. Is solitude one of your natural habitats?
4. Do you continually see stories in life, in yourself, in others around you?
5. Do you have an innate story sense? Do you love a story?
6. Does the recording of life's events seem important to you? Are you saying to other people, "Put it down"?

Perhaps your skills, discovered or undiscovered, lie in weaving, woodwork, ceramics, leather or metal craft, mosaics, sewing, mechanics, photography, gardening or cooking.

Walter Knott of Knott's Berry Farm in Buena Park, California, which grosses several million dollars annually, left a farm in the Mojave Desert where he couldn't make enough to support his four children and moved to Buena Park. He was past 40 at the time, but he took out a loan to buy a 10-acre farm where he raised boysenberries to sell at a roadstand. Mrs. Knott made berry pies and biscuits. People came back for more. And more. Encouraged, Mrs. Knott began to serve chicken dinners. Mr. Knott added as additional attractions myna birds, and an exhibit of candy making. Little by little the two, through imagination and hard work transformed the 10 acres into one of the most famous recreation centers in California.

A friend has found sitting at her sewing machine making

over 600 quilts for destitute people around the world to be an adventure. "It's a new skill," she admits, "but one I am enjoying very much."

Does political service appeal to you? Harry S. Truman's haberdashery business collapsed when he was 40. He ran for and was elected county judge. Although he had only a high school education, he ran for the U.S. Senate when he was 60, and at 61 succeeded Roosevelt as president. He won the office in his own right at 64.

What can you do?

*If you like to travel, you can go places you have never been before.* If you have worked long enough to earn a sizeable chunk of vacation time, consider swapping homes during your vacation and going places where otherwise you couldn't afford to stay. There are bureaus that will make arrangements for a fee, and investigate character and credit of those who use their services. Check with your travel agent.

*If you love to learn* you can enroll in an adult education class, complete the college education you always have wanted, construct your family's genealogy, engage in research, make the acquaintance of the great people of the world by reading their biographies, attend Bible classes either in your neighborhood, at your church or at church colleges, Bible schools or seminaries.

If health allows, *take up a new sport:* golf, fishing, flying, boating, camping, bowling, hiking.

*If you are disabled or confined to a wheel chair most of the time,* get your adventure through quality TV and radio programs, or stereo recordings. Invite friends in. Teach a class in your home. Try some adventures in thinking. Dare to read books you haven't read before. Listen to the points of view of people who differ from you. Take up bird watching.

*If you are temporarily unemployed* you may be able to develop an idea you have been tossing around in your mind for a long time.

Charles Darrow lost his job at 45. Whiling away his time at home, he invented Monopoly. The middle years' love of comfort motivated Anton Lorenz, a teacher of history and geography in Hungary, to design the Barcalounger Reclining Chair. Millions have been sold. Castro wanted both beauty and comfort. He designed his first graceful looking sofa bed when he was 43.

*Trusting the Lord to give you victory in areas where you have often suffered defeat can be an adventure.* It's a great feeling of accomplishment to finally master a mood or habit that has been controlling you. Even taking off excess pounds can be an adventure.

*Sometimes adventure comes as a person begins a new work.* By the time persons are 40, if not earlier, they should know whether or not their work is satisfying enough for them to want to continue it for another 25 years. If it isn't, they are well advised to make a change.

"Worse than illness," Dr. Thomas Holmes, University of Washington professor of psychiatry, states, "is to go on in an intolerable, dull, or demeaning situation."

Even when one's work is enjoyable, the call can come to begin another vocation. Albert Schweitzer was almost 40 when he arrived in Africa as a missionary doctor. When someone questioned his move which involved leaving the concert recital halls of Europe behind, he replied, "I consider myself too blessed and feel called to bring a candle of learning to the darkness."

When George Norman arrived in Lakewood, California, to take up a pastorate in a church there, a local newspaper welcomed him with: "Rookie Pastor of 50 Comes to Lakewood."

Norman was a businessman in Long Island, New York, when he began to consider making a change. His work at the time frequently demanded action on his part that he felt was not morally right. How long could he continue to live a weekday life that was in violation of his own convictions? A bout with pneumonia flattened him and gave him even more time to ponder his situation. When he finally recovered, he resigned, packed up his family, left his lucrative position and moved to California. There he quickly found a new job and a new church home. His family became charter members in a mission church where the pastor began to call on Norman to assist him with the Sunday service and with other responsibilities. Norman discovered he was enjoying his new responsibilities immensely. He again was called on to act dishonestly in his business dealings. This led him to seriously consider a change. His pastor called an ad for a business administrator for a large church to his attention. Norman applied and was hired. He plunged into his work, little realizing it was the prelude to an even more challenging venture.

His father died. Norman went back east for the funeral. A seminar for directors of Christian education was being held in the city and Norman attended some of the sessions. As he visited with some of the people present, they urged him to consider theological training.

Norman was then 47 years old. His family included two pre-teenagers. To take this step would mean forfeiting, once again, hospitalization and pension benefits. His wife encouraged him, reminding him that as an experienced secretary, she would be able to supplement their income. His children insisted they could do without some things, including a new bicycle. Norman enrolled in seminary several hours away, which meant he needed to live away from his family.

But "hitting the books" was not easy for one who had been away from them for 30 years. Norman discovered that he was five years older than his roommate's father! He also found out that while his young fellow students could stay up all hours and enjoy their weekends, and still get by in the classroom, he had to study for hours—and even then he was failing! Greek was the most formidable hurdle. Discouraged, he told himself if he failed one more Greek exam, he would quit. Strangely enough, he began to receive passing grades. The corner was turned. He could handle the return to academic life.

His troubles were not, however, ended. His wife was involved in an automobile accident that totalled their car. When Norman drove 175 miles to bring her their second car, he found that back on the campus he was unable to seek employment because he had no car.

Norman's heart struggle at this time was great. He asked himself if he were attempting the impossible. Was he asking his family to pay too dear a price? Was self-aggrandizement his motive after all? His family encouraged him to go on, and he did.

A local business man tempted him to quit the seminary by offering him a job at a very lucrative salary. "God helped me," Norman says simply.

Fifteen years after he entered his first parish, at the time of his retirement, Norman was more sure than ever that he had done the right thing when he decided to change careers midstream in life.

We must admit, however, that usually one does not change vocations requiring such training during the middle years. *Discovering innovative methods to use in one's own work can bring freshness to an old job and zest to living.* Sometimes a *change in attitude* toward our work may be all that is needed. We need to be convinced our job is important, that even though we may work only with things, still the things we produce benefit and serve people. We can discover a ministry among those with whom we work.

One of our sons once worked as errand boy for a large savings and loan company. Some of his friends, who had worked there previously, had quicky tired of the monotony. They complained that the job held little challenge. Dan's response was "I don't mind the work. When I deliver the mail or run errands, I try to see the people to whom I make the delivery. Many of them are so uptight. The business world isn't an easy place to be. Those above can make it really rough for the little guy below. When I see their worried looks, I smile, or give them a pat on the back and tell them things will work out somehow and that God loves them and cares. You'd be surprised how many smiles I get in return."

*When we view our jobs as our vocation from God, even menial tasks glow.* "There can be no work," Calvin declared, "however vile or sordid that does not glisten before God, and is

not right precious, provided that in it we serve our vocation . . . .
Every person . . . in his or her place ought to dream that this
estate is, as it were, a station assigned to him or her by God."

Brother Lawrence, who wrote the now classic *Practicing the
Presence of God*, in washing pots and pans rubbed and scoured
and polished their bottoms so every pan became a beaming,
happy face, and the presence of God filled the rectory kitchen.

E. Stanley Jones at his *ashrams* in India demonstrated by example the nobility of *all* work. Participants at the ashrams
signed up for various household chores. Jones frequently chose
to empty the wastebuckets from the latrines.

*Many find new zest and interest in life as they plunge into
volunteer work.* Sometimes the volunteer work will open the
door to a position of responsibility. This was true for Beverly
Peterson of Van Nuys, California. She tells her story.

"When I answered the telephone one Monday afternoon
in November I had no idea that this was the beginning of my
adventure in saying 'yes.' The Director of Volunteers of
Pacoima Memorial Lutheran Hospital was calling. 'Could I give
four hours a week to work at the hospital?' she asked. My
children were in school. Why not?

"I was assigned to the Director of Nursing Services and
found myself engulfed in making stencils for nursing procedures, running the mimeograph and assembling manuals. As I
typed, I sometimes saw ideas that could be clarified by re-
statement. I made suggestions. Often my revision would show
up in the final copy.

"I sought to become more useful and continued at the
hospital for eight years.

"During this period I said 'yes' again when someone asked
if I would stand for nomination as a district assembly chairperson for the women's organization of our church. That 'yes'
opened the door to many wonderful friendships. Visits and letters from others widened my horizons. Opportunities for
leadership training presented themselves also. Soon I was con-
ducting dozens of one day workshops. Although I suffered
from butterflies in my stomach at the beginning of each work-

shop, before it was over I found I was enjoying what I was doing.

"After each workshop I carefully reviewed the written evaluations prepared by the workshop participants, being appreciative of the constructive criticisms and encouraged by the compliments as I sought to improve the next presentation.

"Soon I was serving on the larger unit executive board of our women's organization. This brought more training experience, opportunities to participate in program planning and to help develop and write materials for workshop presentations.

"Our children were now approaching college age. We needed to supplement our family income. So it seemed like an answer to our need when John C. Simmons, hospital administrator of Golden State Community Mental Health Center, asked if I would be interested in a position as administrative assistant. I laughed. "Everything I know about the mental health field you can put in a thimble and still have room left over for your finger,' I told him.

"He explained that my primary responsibility would be to work towards developing better communication and working relationships between various departments and personnel. A catalyst between people. A mediator? I wondered if I could be effective in this new role. The administrator seemed to think so. So again I said yes.

"It wasn't long before I was offered another position with a fine mental health center in Los Angeles. Their newly hired Administrator and I had worked together in the past and she thought I could fill an open administrative position and by working together once again we could really make a difference. I looked forward to this new challenge. It also provided an opportunity to assist my husband to reenter the work situation. He had been through two cornea transplants, the first one having been rejected, and had been on disability for some months. His employment was a short distance from the Mental Health Center which meant we could drive to and from work together. My driving would relieve some stress until he was established again in the daily routine of working and could take on the pressure of freeway driving. This change seemed a fortuitous opportunity for both of us.

"On my first day I walked into the center with confidence, quite sure that I could handle whatever came along, for after all, I had weathered many a storm at Golden State. What neither I nor my friend knew was that at the center there was considerable competition among four minority groups. At that time the last thing any of them wanted was a white woman in the position I was hired to fill. Each group desired to fill administrative positions and to obtain favorable care for their own members. Neither of these goals is wrong in itself; however, the manner in which some attempts were made to achieve them was questionable.

"It wasn't long before I became aware of pressure to remove me. Certain individuals were assigned to observe me and my actions. It was disconcerting, to say the least, to have someone standing beside my desk while I was on the phone, or talking with one of my staff, or talking with a patient, and so forth. I realized suddenly that I was getting a first hand lesson in discrimination. As the pressure built I began to think about resigning. But then I would be giving in . . . and 'they' would win! Besides my husband still needed my help.

"I'm not a quitter. I decided to stay for one year. There were many, many times when I prayed, 'Lord, help me get through the next fifteen minutes.' The fifteen minutes would pass, and then I'd pray, 'Lord, thank you, but could you please help me get through the next fifteen minutes? Don't let me cry, help me to be strong.' I grew very close to God during this time. I know I could not have managed without his presence.

"My experiences weren't all negative. As the pressure increased, and the tactics became more obvious, individuals would come to me and quietly say they didn't agree with how I was being treated, or they admired my strength even when I protested that I didn't feel strong. However, in group situations I had no defender, no one to speak for me. I was truly alone . . . except I had the Lord to see me through this most difficult year of my life.

"One day I received a phone call from one whom I had won over. The eventual result of that call was a job offer for the position I hold today with a noted cardiologist. I remember that after our interview I drove home singing. Yet if I had not had that year of experience I would not have been in the position to have qualified for the work I now do.

"As I look back over my life, I can see how each experience has been a preparation for the next. Stick-to-it-iveness, I have discovered, goes a long way. Education and training often can be gained on the job. In addition, courses and seminars are helpful

"Saying 'yes' has broadened my horizons. I shall always be glad I have accepted each challenge as it has come.

"Of course one does not venture out like this alone. My husband and family were always ready to give a word of encouragement. I was always conscious of God with me, aiding me and strengthening me. This has meant more than anything else to me, for I do want to be his witness in whatever work I do."

"The tragedy of life is not so much what men suffer as what they miss," Thomas Carlyle affirmed.

Beverly was able to regard each opportunity that others presented to her as a call to adventure, a call to take the plunge and venture out to do something she wasn't sure she could do, a call to develop new skills.

As we have reiterated before, the middle years with the interests and skills we develop then are extremely important and significant in determining the direction our life will take during our last decades.

Bernice and Dan Condit's story clearly illustrates this. Doors to the world beyond the United States were opened for this Lafayette, California, couple when Bernice's parents gave them their first overseas trip to Europe in 1954. Dan was 45. The trip for them was like trying to eat just one peanut. Four years later they took off again, and they were on their way again four years after that. Only two years elapsed between the next two trips. From 1967 on the trips became yearly events, and each year found them venturing farther and farther afield. Sometimes they took their son, Phil, and his friends or other relatives with them.

Bernice began to work for a traveling consulting business. She became an agent for Europe by Car, a car rental and purchase company.

As they traveled they took pictures to document their visits. Dan had been taking color slides since he was 31. At that time he gave Bernice his pocket camera, and she began to shoot black and white photos. Dan developed them in the darkroom of their home.

A fall trip by car through Hungary, Rumania, Bulgaria, Greece, Turkey, and Yugoslavia went well. It gave the courage to respond positively to an invitation from physician friends to help them in their medical clinics in the Hindu Kush mountains in Afghanistan the summer of 1970. They slept in tents at 9,000 feet elevations. Bernice, with the help of an Afghan cook and a teenage Afghan helper, saw that meals were provided for the team of 25 to 30. Dan, a research chemist, worked in the lab and served as camp chaplain and manager. Whenever Dan and Bernice could grab a few minutes away from their assigned jobs, they used their cameras.

After they returned to the U.S., they disappeared into their darkroom from which they emerged blinking from time to time to speak and show their pictures in churches. They developed their film and sent copies of the pictures back to Afghanistan. That did it.

Requests for more and more copies of their photos poured in. Dan looked at Bernice, and Bernice looked at Dan. Was it possible, they asked each other, that they could serve the church in its overseas mission by taking pictures? Dan was 60. Wouldn't enjoying the health they had which in turn would enable them to become volunteer public relations people for missions mean more to them than a few thousand dollars stored in a bank? They prayed. Dan asked for an early retirement.

That fall Dan was asked to serve on the trustee board of the Bible and Medical Missionary Fellowship. When Bernice heard that the International Director would be visiting in their area she invited him to their home. In the course of the evening they asked him if they volunteered their services, would BMMF be interested in their photographing the work in Nepal? Certainly! he said.

That marked the beginning of 15 years that have encompassed 12 trips photographing the work of 43 missions in 55 countries by this lithe, lean, and radiantly alive couple.

In addition to providing pictures to the various mission organizations Dan and Bernice have found other uses for their photographs. Paragon Production of Campus Crusade for Christ incorporated about 100 of Dan's slides in the multimedia production, "God's Tapestry," used originally at the Conference for Itinerant Evangelists in Amsterdam in 1983. That same summer Bernice exhibited black and white enlargements of some of her work in the museum of the Billy Graham Center in Wheaton, Illinois. Subsequently the exhibit has traveled to Tennessee and California to be used at mission conferences. Youth for Christ used a number of Dan's slides in a media production for their Triennial Convocation in Hong Kong in 1984. In 1985 Pharos Studio in Princeton, N.J., purchased rights to copy 172 of Dan's slides to be used for a presentation they are preparing for the Presidents' Forum V of Pfizer Pharmaceutical Company.

Isn't it risky and dangerous traveling in countries where uneasy and unstable political situations could erupt any time? "Of course," the Condits say in a matter-of-fact way. "That's part of it."

They recall how as they were leaving Calcutta during the time of the trouble between East and West Pakistan they saw workers stacking sandbags around airplanes and positioning guns between the runways. "We were relieved to be airborne," Dan says. Two days later in Bangkok they bought a newspaper. The headlines jumped out at them: "Calcutta Airport Bombed."

In Egypt they were fortunate to get one of the last flights out of Cairo just before the war with Israel began. They heard that after their plane took off there were no flights for weeks.

In Guatemala Bernice's blood pressure soared when an army helicopter opened fire on the Missionary Aviation plane in which she was flying.

In the Bird's Head of Irian Jaya a violent thunderstorm overtook their frail helicopter. "The blinding flashes of lightning and the deafening crashes of thunder really got to me," Bernice admits. "That night I was still so tense that all my toes cramped."

Bernice can list 21 different types of vehicles they have used—in addition to their legs—ranging from dugout canoes to overnight sleeper trains. In developed areas they favor renting a car and they stay in village inns which are cheaper than hotels in big cities. "And more picturesque and interesting," Bernice adds. They picnic frequently. They buy serviceable, easy-to-launder, comfortable clothing.

A secondary interest of the Condits has been entertaining students and visitors from overseas as often as they can. One Taiwanese student, studying at the University of Califonia, Berkeley, appreciated their hospitality so much that he asked them to help him plan his wedding. Dan and Bernice served as parents for the bridal couple and hosted a reception for them. The Condits later were asked to name two of their children. Both the husband and wife have earned doctorate degrees and hold good positions. "Our son lives 800 miles away," Bernice says, "so on holidays we are glad we can have our Taiwanese family with us. They are very special to us and have added an extra dimension to our life." She pauses for a moment, then adds, "It is thrilling to look back over our lives and see how the Lord has led us step by step into pleasant places as we have trusted him. Praise his name."

The need for adventure continues to be basic throughout our lives. We are explorers at heart. True satisfaction will come, not through exploration in fields that are morally out-of-bounds, but in response to the rightful demands society places on us; not in passively viewing the adventures of others, but by our own plunging into ventures; not even in development of innate gifts solely for the joy and satisfaction of development, but in using those gifts to serve the larger community.

Jesus calls us to adventure with him. The words in which he clothes his invitation may sound strange to our ears, but deep within ourselves we know he is speaking the truth. We feel the tug at our hearts and want to respond.

He declares: "Unless a grain of wheat falls into the earth and dies, it remains alone; but if it dies, it bears much fruit. He who loves his life loses it, and he who hates his life in this world will keep it for eternal life. If any one serves me, he must follow me, and where I am, there shall my servant be also" John 12:24-26).

If we will let God lead us, he will take us down new roads and open new vistas. All other adventures will pale before the royal adventure of following Jesus as our Lord and as Lord of Lords. Just when we thought life was becoming dull and commonplace we will discover instead that it throbs with new, unexpected surprises, a promise of the best yet to come

## For Thought and Discussion

1. If a person sees, on careful reflection, that he or she *has* a good job, why not appreciate it, even celebrate it? If, on the other hand, it checks out as a bad job, why not improve it or determine to quit?

Sometimes jobs can be enhanced through restructuring. Sometimes they can't. Anyone considering quitting his or her present job may be helped by answering the following questions:

1. Is the company unfair or unfeeling?
2. Do jobs to which I could advance appeal to me?
3. Do your superiors give you the message that they expect you to fail? (You will.)
4. Do you drag to work or stay home on the slightest excuse?
5. Are you stoking yourself with coffee or pep pills or numbing yourself with drugs or alcohol?
6. Have you recently begun flaring out in anger or sulking and giving others the silent treatment?

7. Do you suffer from aches and pains for which your doctor can find no physical reason?

8. Have you tried adopting a positive attitude toward your work plus increasing your times of recreation and rest and still find no improvement in how you feel about your work?

Middle-aged people usually are extremely reluctant to quit a job. They don't want to lose pension or retirement benefits or come up against discriminatory hiring practices. They also fear the unknown.

Actually, it's foolish to run away from something without having something to run to. The worker who proposes to make a change should consider some questions:

1. Is he or she suited for the new activity being contemplated?

2. Will preparation be required?

3. Are positions available?

2. Life has many dimensions besides work. To understand how we are spending our time after work, answering the following questions might be helpful:

1. Think back over the decisions made this past week in your family. How were they made? What were priorities?

2. Do your children's activities seem in tune with your interests or at variance with what you think is important?

3. Have you ever made a personal list of priorities in regard to: places to go; people to invite; things to do; interests to develop?

4. Has your family done this?

5. To what extent should the fact that you are a Christian have an effect on the priorities and decisons you make?

3. Do you belong to organizations? The next questions may help you evaluate as to which ones you should give yourself.

1. The most dynamic organization to which I belong is . . .

2. My responsibilities in that organization are . . .

3. The purpose of the organization is . . .

4. Other purposes ought to be . . .

5. In the past year I have been influential in effecting the following changes in that organization . . .
6. The organization is of the following benefit in my family's life . . .
7. The organization is of the following benefit in our church family . . .
8. The organization is of the following benefit to the community in which I live . . .

4. Complete the following statements:

"I think I am essential to my family because . . . "

"I think I am essential to my church because . . . "

"I think I am essential to my community because . . . "

"I think I am essential to my God because . . . "

5. Suppose you have retired. How, specifically, can you schedule next week?

Make a chart which will allow you to schedule one major activity for the morning, afternoon, and evening of each day of the week. Then fill in the blank spaces.

If you have trouble filling in all the empty spaces, or if too many of the blanks are filled with the same kinds of activities, perhaps you had better take a second look at how you are living your life now, how you are spending your time, and what interests you are developing.

## 11

# Special Demands of Autumn and Winter

> *Does the road wind uphill all the way?*
> *Yes, to the very end.*
> *Will the day's journey take the whole long*
>    *day?*
> *From morn to night, my friend.*
> —Christina Georgina Rossetti

Shakespeare described seven stages of life in this way: infants, school children, lovers, soldiers, travelers, leaders in development; he then defined the last span of life as being one in which we are guardians of the soul of the nation.

## Our Responsibility Defined

Leaders in development. Guardians of the soul of the nation. These are awesome responsibilities.

For Christians the phrases can suggest additional unique responsibilities: leaders in development of Christ's mission and concern for our own relationship to God and also the relationship of others to God.

Christians are concerned about the hurts, ills, injustices and problems of this present world. We also believe that life does not end with the grave. We believe too that the quality of the life we shall have after the resurrection will be determined here and now, by our faith and attitudes or unbelief toward God and all that God offers. Christians see themselves and all others of double value. As mortals we are of value now, yet because we are immortal as well, we all shall have value in eternity, that mysterious realm about which we know so little but of which the Bible speaks so confidently. Christians are concerned about *both* the present life and the life to come.

Someone has described the middle years as the "Command Generation." That is, we make the decisions, we carry the major portion of responsibilities. How are we doing the job?

*Some shirk responsibility.* They assume as little responsibility as possible. When confronted with larger needs, they have many reasons for not becoming involved. Let us consider some of the reasons given and ask if they are valid.

*I'm not responsible for the problems that exist; it's not my fault.*
"Middle-agers are like Mexican burros," an article in *Changing Times* stated. "They carry an incredible load and receive a good many kicks to boot."

Many feel this way. As they see it, they are paying heavy taxes and doling out a major share of college expenses and then are accused of being slaves to a work ethic. They have worked for better living conditions, provided medical care for their families, contributed to medical research, and have had families half or even one-fourth the size of their predecessors, yet they are told they have caused the overpopulation of the world. They provide comfortably for their families and are told their affluent living has brought on the ecological crisis. They are either immigrants themselves or children of immigrants, but they are blamed for all the injustices done to blacks, Indians, Hispanics, and migrant workers and illegal aliens.

"I've had it—up to here!" said one, drawing a swift line under his chin. "If I hear one more word about Indians, I'll punch someone in the nose."

"I refuse, absolutely refuse, to feel guilty about problems which have their roots in another century," another said heatedly.

Because of all the accusations hurled at them, many in their middle years feel unappreciated, misunderstood, and unduly blamed for problems they alone did not cause. Their reaction is to withdraw.

Can we say we are not guilty? Even though we personally may not be responsible for the major world problems that exist, because we are members of the human race, are we not corporately guilty?

This does not mean we have to be weighed down with guilt. We make clear our penitence by doing what we can to correct the wrong that has been done. We may need to change some aspect of our lifestyle. We accept God's forgiveness. But we acknowledge our guilt, our anger, and our bias to ourselves and to others; we do not defensively deny it.

*"Why should I contribute? Funds are mishandled."*

"India? Why should I be concerned about India's poverty when I learn how much they squander on nuclear weapons? And so what if people are dying of hunger? Thank God a few are dying, or we'd all soon be dead."

In many cases cynicism and disillusionment are hatching lethargy, indifference, callousness, or resignation.

As Christians are we not sons and daughters of One who causes the sun to shine on the just and unjust? Do we not follow One who contributed to a corruption-ridden priesthood system at the same time that he worked for reform? Do we not benefit daily from the gifts God pours out on us, whether we deserve them or not—or misuse them? And do not enough reliable denominational and private agencies exist so we can channel our help through them?

*"I've done my part."*

"Of course, I'm concerned. But we've worked hard and done our part. Someone younger can take over. It's only fair we should get to enjoy ourselves now. Fishing, boating, camping, traveling. We haven't had a chance to do this before. What's wrong with that?"

And so the route to self-indulgence is taken.

We need to ask ourselves if the resources at our disposal are really ours to use for selfish purposes, or are they a trust gifted to us by God to be shared with those less fortunate than we? Is wealth a reward, or a responsibility? Is it entrusted to us to provide security for ourselves or is it given us as resources to be used? And can we be truly happy just "doing what I've always wanted to do" when it reflects a life turned in upon itself? In due time, won't travel become commonplace, fishing monotonous, camping a chore? Won't the highest in us begin to stir up restless longing and dissatisfaction demanding that we do something purposeful again? Or have we succeeded completely in dulling that sensitivity?

Dag Hammarskjold entered in his diary this personal reflection: "You have not done enough, you have never done enough, so long as it is still possible that you have something of value to contribute."

Justice Holmes extended the age of assuming responsibility when on his 90th birthday he remarked: "The riders in a race do not stop short when they reach the goal. There is a little finishing canter before coming to a standstill. There is time to hear the kind voices of friends and to say to one's self, 'The work is done.' But just as one says that, the answer comes: 'The race is over, but the work is never done while the power to work remains.' To live is to function. That is all there is to living."

*"The problem is too complicated for me; I don't understand it and I wouldn't know what to do."*

Some problems seem so gigantic, so snarled, so hopeless that our reaction may be to push a button and tune out that which disturbs us.

Famine. Disease. Intense social unrest. Injustice. Violence. War. The seeds have sprouted. The crisis overhangs the world. It is not being faced realistically, and perhaps one reason is because it scares us to death to do so!

In self-defense, we rationalize. We say other people could make it as we did if they would try. We declare there *are* enough world resources for all of us to live as comfortably as we do (and perhaps there are, if distribution were fair).

We try to escape by consoling ourselves with the thought that all these are signs of the end times, that Jesus is coming soon, and all our troubles will be over. To look for the return of the Lord Jesus *is* the Christian's joyous, sustaining hope, but Christ never meant that expectancy to be the fire escape we take from the burning building. He wants us to be fire-fighters, not escapees.

Or we leave the problem to someone else to solve—we don't know who specifically, but someone—there must be someone. Maybe a government agency?

The fact is that the worldwide problems of just one issue—say food—are so enormous that to solve it calls for the accumulated, extensive experience of the most astute minds of the world and for the willingness to cooperate on the part of each of us, where we are, doing what we *can* do. To shirk this responsibility, to leave the solutions to our children, not only would be cruel, but immoral.

*Some do not support their stated priorities by the actual way in which they expend time, energy, and resources.*

Some of us declare ourselves responsible for certain areas with our lips, but our lives do not support our declarations. We are living double lives.

For example, we rate a good marriage and a happy home high on our priority list, yet actually we give very little time, thought or effort to bringing this about. We are caught between loyalty to family and loyalty to job or career and feel torn. We respond most often to the one that brings in the money, and then feel guilty because we do so.

Again we try to rationalize our way out saying it is not the *quantity* of time we give, but the *quality* that is important, forgetting that rarely can we have quality without quantity. The classic works of art which have endured down through the years, the paintings, the sculpture, the literature, the music masterpieces, all have demanded enormous investments of time.

Also, the very fact that we have limited time often erodes

the quality of the time that we do have. Take the working parents' relationship to their children for example. Harried and overburdened with responsibilities both within and without the home, the little time spent with their family is often characterized by tension, pressure, haste, worry, and short-temperedness.

This is not always the case, of course. Some persons seem to thrive on huge loads of responsibility and rise to it and actually become better individuals.

In many cases a limited amount of time to give to the family means a lower quality in the personal relationship extended during that time also. We give our children extravagant allowances to make up for it and salve our consciences or spend excessive amounts on elaborate wardrobes for them, or allow them to participate in every activity their schools offer and their friends coax them to join in—regardless of the cost. We need to be sure that in doing this we are not actually injuring the ones we love the most.

Or again, we profess to be Christians but give minimal time to nurturing our spiritual lives or reaching out to others in need. We need to ask ourselves if our use of our time and energy truly reflects our professed priorities.

*Some experience conflict between responsibility to themselves as persons against responsibility to others.*

Recently I heard of a man who studied to become a minister. But he was not the kind of a minister his mother had hoped he would be. So he became a youth worker in a large church. He was not the success at being a youth worker his mother had expected he would be. Now he is raising cacti. On the front and back of his sweat shirt he has two signs which read, "How am I doing, Ma?" and "I'm really trying, Ma."

Some arrive at their middle years still caught in the bind of trying to be someone other than who they are. A distorted sense of responsibility to others imprisons them, forcing them to try to fit into roles that are repulsive to them. They have never promised themselves—and then acted on that promise—that first and foremost they will be true to themselves.

Even those who are trying to live out lives that reflect their true selves need to continue to be aware of the need of assuming responsibility for themselves. This might mean as simple an act as a busy mother's feeling free to take one day a week off for her own personal recreation, renewal, and refreshment. For parents it might mean spending money to enrich and enhance their own inner lives instead of heaping all the privileges on their children. When Jesus commanded us to love our neighbors as ourselves, he was not scorning the importance of self-love, but rather underlining it. In order to act responsibly toward others, we must be free to care for ourselves as persons.

*Some permit themselves to be driven compulsively by an overwhelming sense of responsibility to an amazing array of needs.*

At the other end of the balance scale from those who shirk responsibility we find those harried, tense souls who rush around from one meeting to another, who add project to project until at last they collapse on a hospital bed with ulcers or a heart attack. They have not learned to come to grips with reality. They *are* limited. They cannot meet every need. They also have not learned to trust others with responsibility. And they have not learned to delineate between the difference of remaining sensitive and open to all need without feeling compelled to respond personally to each call for help.

### A More Acceptable Way to Handle Responsibility.

Jesus points the way for us to respond to need. He saw need on a much wider scope than we ever do. The bruises and wounds of those he loved twisted and knotted his stomach. As he pointed out need to his followers, he also told them how to respond. "The harvest is plenteous," he said. "The fields are white. But the laborers are few. Pray, therefore, the Lord of the harvest that he will thrust forth laborers into the harvest." (Luke 10:2)

An appropriate and effective response to overwhelming need is not to shirk it, not to shut it out, not to become calloused or indifferent, not to lose our joy through a sense of frustration, not to walk around with a burdened, hangdog look because of guilt, but rather to respond by turning over the need to God. He is far more concerned than we. We ask him to fill the needs, to call forth workers. Of course, as we pray we shall hold ourselves open to anything he has to say to us.

Let us touch on four guidelines which may help us know what God is calling us to do.

## Sensing Which Needs Require Our Response

*Guideline 1.* We have to be convinced the need actually exists.

A well-known author and his wife, observing their lives and conversation, came to the conclusion that many of their relatives were not Christians. So they began to pray for them, loved them, helped them as there was opportunity, and spoke to them about their relationship to Christ. The result was, when I heard last, 28 of their relatives definitely had committed their lives to Christ.

The beginning of that ministry was the acceptance of the fact that the relatives needed to come to Christ personally. The awareness was then followed by action.

*Guideline 2.* Sometimes other people will call to our attention a need to which we can respond.

This was true of Bert and Mary of Los Angeles. It all began when their daughter, Sharon, after a year and a half in college, came home and announced, "I want to get away and think. I'm going to Mexico Saturday. There's an orphanage there where I want to work."

Sharon went on to tell her parents about the Christian couple who had taken in one or two homeless waifs first, and then more and more children had come until they had more to care for than they could manage on their own. With mixed feelings Mary watched Bert and Sharon drive off on Saturday. When Bert came back, she questioned him and then said, "I want to go and see for myself."

Those who have crossed the U.S. border into Baja, California, know the depressed feeling that comes when confronted by the realities of miserable shacks, mud roads, and bare, windswept hills. Poverty seems everywhere.

"As we drove into the yard of the orphanage, my heart sank," Mary recalls. "The sickly, sweet smell of urine greeted us. As a nurse I guessed the smell was coming from more than the outdoor privies, and later I found I was right. The children who had been mistreated before coming to the orphanage were wetting their beds."

" 'You need plastic mattress covers,' I said to Sharon. 'No money, Mom,' she said."

"On the way home my heart was perplexed. 'Lord,' I prayed, 'I know we gave our daughter to you, but why did you have to send her to such a place,' And do you know what the Lord answered me? He said, 'Quit your belly-aching and get down there and help her.'

"Shortly after, I addressed a women's gathering. I told them about the need of the orphanage. Good used mattresses were donated. I sewed plastic mattress covers with muslin backing that slipped on like pillow cases. Then we loaded the car with food and the mattresses and again visited the orphanage. Oh, how grateful they were! You see, they had had only beans for three weeks.

"Word spread about the orphanage. Members from one of our churches visited it. They asked Sharon what her most immediate need was. She rolled up the sleeves of her blouse. Her arms were peppered with large, red welts. 'Bedbugs,' she said simply. 'Can you do anything about them?'

"They hired a Mexican firm to fumigate once a month and got rid of the bugs. The church also supplied wool blankets, toilets, heaters, a bathtub, food, clothing, and much more.

"My husband collected and repaired old washing machines. I collected used clothing. Many church people and groups became interested. It was thrilling to see needs met and improvements taking place. For almost two years every spare hour of ours was poured into the orphanage. Then our daughter felt she should return to college for further training.

Individuals and groups still help the orphanage, and the work continues. How grateful we are for the experience we had! We've never been the same since, and we wouldn't have missed it for anything."

Sharon uncovered the need for her parents, and they, in turn, were able to communicate the need to others.

*Guideline 3.* Often God makes his will clear to us through open and closed doors.

Edner and Fern Holmen, a farming couple in Butterfield, Minnesota, cherished an intense interest in missions. This led to their beginning to prepare with further training and offering themselves for service overseas. When Fern's heart condition closed the door for them they turned back to their 273-acre mortgaged farm and waited on God for further directions. As they did they plunged into the work of their local church— youth work, Sunday School, family nights, women's organization, church council. Somehow, in addition to caring for their three children, Fern and Edner found time to help with all. But they longed to do more. Why couldn't they be farmers for the Lord and their living be for giving?

The result has been that for the last three and a half decades Fern and Edner have given one-fourth or more of their income to the work of the Lord, with the largest portion going to missions. The total has amounted to over $127,000. Even the first lean years of their marriage did not discourage them from giving, in fact, it was experiencing God's faithfulness then that enabled them to venture out to give more and more.

They have discovered also the gift of hospitality. Missionaries and youth teams passing through their area always find a warm welcome, hearty meals and comfortable beds ready for them at Holmens.

When their children entered high school Fern and Edner began to have youth meetings in their home every other Saturday night. They would sing, study the Bible together, eat and have fun. When Judy went away to college she came back for those Saturday night meetings and brought a couple of cars full of students with her. "They'd bring sleeping bags and stay over till Sunday night," Fern remembers.

At these Saturday night meetings they were able to reach out to many in acute need. One young girl who had been attending was shot and killed by her brother as she was pleading with him to give up the occult world where he had become active. The parent's response, however, was unexpected. They volunteered for missionary service and are in Africa today.

As people have learned of the Holmen's interest in missions and discovered how well informed they are they have invited them to speak in churches and at camps and conferences. Little by little Edner has enlarged his speaking to include other subjects also such as stewardship, salvation, evangelism, and world hunger.

Six years ago the Holmens volunteered to organize and manage a family weekend at a camp grounds to better inform people about the work done by a mission organization they support. A pastor who attended one year became so interested and supportive that this led to his being elected to the governing board of the mission.

Edner recalls a youth conference where he had offered an elective seminar. "Very few came," he says, "but a doctor did. As a result he served overseas for a year as an associate missionary. He too is now on the board of the mission. And last summer when we were visiting in Iowa I talked with a young man, and he is now working in Bolivia."

Edner and Fern, though they are far-sighted enough to see the whole world still are near-sighted enough to see those around them too.

"We share the good news of Jesus with all who come to our door," Edner says. "When sales persons come, I can get in two, three hours talking about the Lord." He chuckled. "Once a tire salesman even knocked off $75 from our bill because he said our conversation had been so helpful."

Giving books and tapes has been another way Fern and Edner reach out.

We see how closed doors to one area of service for the Holmens opened many other doors even wider.

*Guideline 4.* When we say we are open to all needs but respond to "opportunities at hand," we mean opportunities that we have the skills and abilities to meet.

John and Polly Holloway were in their forties when they went to Tanzania, East Africa. In addition to years of business experience, John had a CPA certificate and an understanding of the Bible that had come through fourteen Bible correspondence courses. John used his skills to work as a business manager and field treasurer for a large African church, and in his spare time he preached, taught and started a church.

After four years in Tanzania they went to Ecuador to oversee the finances of a large school built mainly with a grant from West Germany's Bread for the World funds. John started a church in Ecuador too.

John and Polly are quick to acknowledge they couldn't have accomplished what they have without the loyal support of their home congregation. The combined abilities and resources of the Holloways and their congregation made it possible for them to respond to opportunities which presented themselves.

*Guideline 5.* We might see need and opportunities for which we presently do not have resources, but that should not deter us. God can provide resources in many ways.

When Art Storhaug of Larkspur, a suburb of San Francisco, wanted to go to Tanzania under World Brotherhood Exchange, he lacked the funds needed to transport his family to Africa. That did not stop Art. He borrowed the needed money. At the end of their term when they flew back to the United States— again on borrowed money—Art's wife, Esther, thought they were back to stay. But as soon as Art had his loan paid off, he offered his services to work in the Tanzania Christian Refugee Service in Dar es Salaam. During the next eight years as Art cared for thousands of refugees that flooded into Tanzania, Esther found joy in teaching the Bible during released time in the schools. She also worked on an occupational therapy project for lepers, launching a garden and chicken program. New life and hope came to the leper patients as they were able to earn an income selling eggs and broiler chickens.

As Art and Esther discovered, we too will experience that as we launch out and use the resources we have, God supplies the ones we need but lack. Changing times and conditions are altering the traditional pattern of mission work. In most places traditional "mission fields" have ceased to exist. The church of Jesus Christ has taken root and is growing. The national churches can be justly proud of the many able, dedicated leaders they have. Christians are assuming support of the work. But need for trained personnel in some areas of work continues to exist. In many instances now the emphasis has shifted to supplying needed personnel for projects of the existing national churches. Intercristo, a computer style service is one service that facilitates the matching of need with personnel.

There is still need for pioneers to reach into difficult areas with the Gospel. If you have a skill you would like to use overseas, contact the personnel director of the overseas work of your denomination or of a mission organization with which you are familiar. Personnel directors can tell you if there are any openings and can guide you as to how to proceed.

### Saying "Yes" Enriches Us

As we in our middle years realize that the "good life" is not to be equated merely with comfort, material possessions, freedom, leisure, or security, we will be freed to act responsibly, which is the essence of assuming responsibility. By-products are satisfaction, inner peace, personal growth, broadened understanding, and a compassionate heart. All of this, even though we may face difficult trials, will make the years ahead some of the best we've had.

### For Reflection and Discussion

1. How can I, as a Christian, act responsibly in regard to myself? My immediate family? My extended family? My

church? My community? My country? The world at large? My Lord and his commands?

2. In Exodus 3 we read about a middle-aged man receiving a call from God. Who was he? What did God call him to do? Why? What background and training did he have that would help him do the job? How had he earlier recognized the need? See Exodus 2:11. What was the difference between his response then and his response when God called him? See Exodus 2:10–15; 3:11–4:1; 10, 13. How did God answer his objections? What lay between the call and the fulfillment of the promise given at the time of the call?

## 12

# Keeping Green As Autumn Fades

> *Maturity: among other things—not to hide one's strength out of fear and, consequently, live below one's best.*
> —Dag Hammarskjold

Our family was seated at the table for dinner. Joining us was a guest, a young man who would graduate from college in a week's time. "Only seven more days," he exulted, "and I'll be free! No more hassle with school or books."

One of our youngsters stared at him, her fork arrested halfway in its journey to her mouth. "No more school?" she asked. "Never?"

"Never!"

She regarded his bright young face with wonder, then looked at our graying heads and shook her head. "Can you beat that?" she said. "I thought people went to school and studied all their lives. My mom and dad do." Luverne and I are, of course, only two of a steadily growing number of adults who find ourselves continually drawn to the classroom.

Psychologists tell us that *one of the needs of middle adulthood is cognitive.* One person explained it this way: "I have a lot more learning facility in middle life than I did when I was in high school and college. I have a desire to learn new things, to read more books, to be creative. I am far more stimulated than I was when I was younger."

Usually we do not think in terms of satisfying a basic human need when we return to school. Instead we are more apt to give other reasons. If we are in business or some profession, the explosion of knowledge we are experiencing makes it necessary for us to take courses periodically in order *to update our skills and not become obsolete.*

*Why are middle-aged persons flocking to the classroom?* Many of those back in school are *preparing themselves for a second or third career.* A retired navy officer we know is employed in an executive position now, but is taking a CPA course in preparation for a third career.

Hundreds of middle-aged students are *women who are preparing themselves for employment outside the home.* No longer content to work as sales clerks or waitresses, they are training to do work they have wanted to do for a long time. "Only one more year, and I'll have my degree in nursing," one radiant woman told me. "The dream of a lifetime is about to be fulfilled."

*Others are thinking ahead to retirement years* when they will have large chunks of time to fill. They are discovering and developing skills and interests in many fields.

*Some study for the love of learning.* Possessed with an eager, inquisitive mind, they are always rejoicing over horizons broadened and the dawning of new understanding. "I never realized before how little I really know," one soon-to-retire business man, who had registered for a number of history courses, told me.

*A few seek companionship and friendship among like-minded people in the classes they attend.* A woman who had just suffered a divorce was enrolled in a psychology class I took. She found the receptive friendliness and concern of her young fellow students healing.

Whatever, their reason, Americans in midlife are on the march back to school, and the doors are wide open. The complaint, "I wish I had been able to get more education," is no longer valid. It's never too late. Even 60- to 80-year-olds are realizing this. Thousands of high schools offer continuing education courses. Colleges and universities across the land welcome the mature student, either as day or night students. Many of them have special weekend or other programs for the "non-traditional student."

New patterns are emerging too. Radio, print, telephone and personal contact are used to bring career education to adults in their homes. There are learning labs, which have programmed materials that users can select to learn at their own pace.

One does not have to go to school in order to learn. Libraries are well-stocked with books, records, tapes and films. In addition, YMCAs, churches, civic groups and other organizations sponsor courses. Many of these are practical, designed to help in the art of living. Courses in marriage and family relationships, money management, and coping with tension or staying well, and of course cooking, are becoming more and more common.

### Going Back to School Full-time

"I might be able to manage a course or two like that," you say, "but to do what I really want to do, I would need to go full-time for four years. Impossible!"

Maybe not. Admittedly it's difficult for a man, although as we mentioned in a previous chapter, George Norman found a way. Other men manage by going to night school several years. If you're a woman whose husband's salary can support the family, it can be done a bit more easily. Oh, it still won't be easy, but the satisfaction gained is usually worth the effort. At least this is what Kay Lee of St. Paul, Minnesota, says. Kay approached middle age with the dissatisfied feeling that she had not accomplished all she had hoped to, that she could do more if only she were better trained.

Before marriage Kay had earned a Bachelor of Sacred Music degree. After college she married a young pastor, Otis Lee. Giving birth to and raising five children as she followed her husband first to Alaska and then to Brazil filled the next 25 years. She filled any spare time with teaching and home study and gloried in both. But she longed for the challenge and discipline of a classroom situation, the insight of an authority and interaction with other learners. A dream she had cherished of teaching kindergarten began to come to life. Training would mean returning to college. "Why not?" Otis said. When the Lees returned to the United States from Brazil and settled in California, both Kay and a son registered as students at Biola College in La Mirada.

Their son lived on campus. With one daughter still in junior high, one in high school, a busy pastor-husband and a bed-ridden mother to care for, Kay commuted the eleven miles from their home three days a week. She applied for and received a student loan through a bank.

"I looked forward to each class hour," Kay says. "History brought a new appreciation of important events of the past. Philosophy opened new vistas of thought. Art appreciation was a joy."

Math was Kay's downfall! Her struggle with basic math produced only a dismal D and brought Kay's grade point average down to a 3.35 when she had hoped for a top score. Kay encountered math again in a statistics course during her third year. The course was required for the psychology major she was now hoping to earn. At first Kay stubbornly said to herself, "If all these kids can do it, I can too." As the classes became increasingly difficult, Kay decided to work around her problem by changing her major to humanities. Immediately she found herself in her element, and each class a challenge and joy.

During Kay's second year at college, her mother died. Kay increased her load to 15 and 18 units a semester. Outside of school Kay narrowed down her life to only the essentials. She included in those "essentials" Sunday school teaching, choir directing, some home visitation, and an hour a week for group Bible study.

Kay's family was supportive. Her married daughters were proud that their mother was at college. Kay found her own understanding widening. New insights provided lines of communication with the growing young adults of their family.

Mealtime conversation was enlivened and food was seasoned with the exchange of ideas that flew across the table. As Kay gained knowledge, her self-confidence grew. At the same time she became more aware of the problems and pressures her children were facing. Her children sensed this and began to express their fears as well as sharing their successes.

On graduation day her family applauded as Kay walked off the stage, not only with her B.A. degree, but with *cum laude* recognition.

A few years later Kay again returned to school. This time she enrolled in a seminary and graduated with a master's degree in divinity. For two and one-half years she and her husband shared a ministry in a four-point parish in North Dakota. "Our skills are complementary," Kay notes.

Kay received a call to serve in the national office of her denomination. She works there with others, preparing materials for congregations in worship and music, evangelism, education, camping and women's ministries. A third of her time is spent visiting congregations in order to understand their needs and sharing these with others in the national office.

**You Can Too**

If you feel God calling you to a particular work but lack the training, take courage from Kay. Knowing what you want, combined with experience, perseverance and patience can see your dream realized. No matter what your needs are, the chances of finding a course are excellent. Check the public library. If you are employed, inquire whether your company will sponsor education for you either through released-time programs or by paying tuition costs.

If you live in a rural community or are a shut-in, you can study by correspondence. Opportunities for discovering and developing our abilities in these middle years never have been as plentiful. Use them!

**For Discussion and Sharing**

If you are using this book in a class setting, ask those in

your group how many have been or are engaged in continuing study. Have them share their experiences with the class.

Have someone in the class research the opportunities that there are for continuing study locally and report. Don't omit opportunities for Christian education. Perhaps there is an instructor or someone from a nearby college or university who could share with the class about educational programs for the older student.

**13**

# Charting My Course:
# Setting Goals

*"A goal is like a magnet. It motivates people, directs their behavior and brings out their best performance."*
—George Haddad

I was sitting on the floor with my young fellow student friends in Psychology 1-A class at Cypress College. Our class had divided into groups to study the different developmental stages of people. The group reporting had chosen to study the middle years. They had conducted surveys, going up and down their blocks asking people questions.

"We asked them what their goals are now," one of the young women said. "Their children are on their own or soon will be. Their home is nearly paid for. They still have several years left before retirement. They seemed surprised. 'Goals? Well, uh . . . ' they stuttered, 'Dunno, hadn't thought much about it. Fish a little, maybe, camp a little, travel a little.' They didn't know really, hadn't thought too much about it."

"We asked them if they were happy," another student reported. "They sort of stared at me when I asked. Happy? Happy? What was happiness? Why, sure they supposed they were happy. Wife hasn't left them yet. Kids married. Job going all right. Nothing great, but bringing in the bucks. Retirement benefits stacking up. Health reasonably good—who doesn't

have a few twinges in the hinges, huh? But considering everything why shouldn't they be happy, huh?"

One of the women interrupted. "I think that they're still all
shook up because they've been left on their own. Kids are gone.
What's there left to live for?"

"I know," one of the young men said thoughtfully. "It's so
sad. There just aren't any of us kids who are worthy of the entire lifetime of two individuals. I mean, if all they have lived for
is us, their children, how can we hope to become so great that
their investment of two entire lives will be justified? Really,
they should have something else to live for besides us. Some
other goals and concerns—especially in this day and age."

I sat silent in my place in the circle, but listened so hard I
was sure my ears, like a rabbit's, must have been poking up
through my hair.

That was the beginning of my inquiry several years ago.
Are the young people correct in their observations, I
wondered? Are we really living without goals? I began to listen,
to ask questions, to read. The final outcome is this book. And
now we have come to the closing chapter, our final visit
together.

We have noted so far that midway through life we
acknowledge, with thankfulness:

—that we are the recipients of bonus years, a longer span
of middle years, replete with opportunities, than has ever been
known before by a generation or civilization

—that God holds out to us the promise of a life that brings
infinite satisfaction

—that research and good living conditions have granted us
better physical health and a longer life expectancy than has ever
been true before

—that much help is available to teach us to cope with and
use tensions and pressures creatively

—that even pain and disability, when encountered and
handled properly, can lead us to fuller lives

—that married life, after 15 or 20 years, can become richer
and happier than it ever has been

—that new relationships with young adult children can bring joy as we experience how rewarding it is to be able to enjoy the delightful people our children have become

—that even if our children bring heartaches, God's sustaining grace is available for us

—that an amazing army of concerned people stand by to help us care lovingly for aging parents

—that, at long last, we are beginning to understand that security, like satisfaction, does not lie in the dollar, but in the unshakeable certainty, based on God's word, that God will never abandon us

—that we have not peaked out—adventure still beckons us, and there are valid ways to satisfy this yen for adventure

—that assuming responsibility will make all we have gone through so far infinitely worthwhile as we find opportunities to use what we have learned and earned

—that it is possible for us to get whatever training we need to accomplish the goals we want to attain

—that we are not left on our own. All the resources of God are available for us. We can live a God-directed, purposeful life with worthwhile, significant goals.

Impressive as this list is, still these facts are not the most important considerations. The most important issue is couched in a question: What are we going *to do* with all this? It won't be September Morning forever.

## Setting New Goals

One of the purposes of this book has been to help us think back over the way we have come, re-evaluate goals we set earlier in life and set new goals for the last halves of our lives.

How can we choose our goals wisely? We can rephrase the question by asking, how can we know God's will and plan for the rest of our lives?

God leads and directs in many ways. May I suggest some directives I have followed as I have sought to understand God's will for my life? Perhaps they will be helpful to you.

Let us note first that as Christians our position is unique.

We may expect God to guide us; therefore, the procedure in arriving at goals or a sense of direction will be different from that found in secular books on the subject.

1. *As a Christian, I shall begin my search by making a commitment or recommitment of myself to God.* I give myself to him. I promise to obey God in whatever I believe he wants me to do.

Often it is helpful to make this commitment in writing; then we are decisive about it. Writing is also useful because then we can return to our written pact with God, reread it and reaffirm our stance during days of temptation and indecision. For your guidance, a suggested statement of commitment is included at the end of this chapter.

Some of us may get hung up on this first step. It is not easy to give ourselves to God. The root of sin, which basically is an independent spirit which desires to live apart from God, is buried deep within us. Selfishly we may be glad to experience the release from guilt which comes when we accept the forgiveness of God. But to surrender *all* our "rights" to God—well, that's a different matter!

To give ourselves entirely to God is difficult also because sin has warped our thinking. In our crooked way we envision God's will for us to be something unpleasant, undesirable, virtually impossible—a cross to be borne. We have a hard time believing God's will for us will be joyous, bringing us the utmost in satisfying fulfillment in life. Because of our warped outlook, we shrink back from  making a commitment of ourselves to God. Such a commitment may not always be simple, or easy.

I was 19 when the Lord showed me how shallow my first commitment to him had been, and how sweeping and inclusive he wanted it to be. It stunned me, frightened me. "If I give God my eyes," I foolishly worried, "suppose he takes my eyesight from me?" Fear controlled me. I needed love to motivate me and trust to take the leap.

Indeed, only as we grow in love and trust of God will we be able to make ever deeper commitments to him. It should be an ongoing process. All too often it isn't.

The flame of devotion and dedication burns white-hot during youth, only to cool off gradually until by midlife we can rationalize the rightness of our choosing to what extent we shall obey God. We become wise in our own discernment. Wedded to security, we are governed by fear instead of being prompted by love. That is why it is good, midway in life, to pause and make a commitment or recommitment of ourselves to Christ. The decisive act should be followed by a day-to-day and hour-to-hour reaffirmation to God and ourselves that Jesus is indeed Lord, and we are his.

So by making a covenant of obedience with God we establish our ultimate goal for life. From there we can move on to receive directions for secondary goals which will be accomplished in longer or shorter periods of time.

In understanding what our secondary goals should be, we need God's guidance. How can we know what to pursue? God guides in many ways.

2. *Pray, be open to the prompting of the Holy Spirit and patiently wait until he speaks to you.* This will require spiritual discipline.

As you pray and wait, answering the following questions should be considered:

What concerns me?

What evidence is there that I should consider each of these concerns to be a concern regarded seriously by me?

Which concerns require *urgent* attention?

Which of these items has become a growing concern for me?

Jot down your answers. Some of these concerns undoubtedly will be for others and some for yourself.

Another question to ask yourself is, what have I long dreamed of doing?

As you are doing this, make out three lists. On one, list all your abilities (don't be falsely modest. God has given you these abilities expecting you to use them.) On one list write down your developed skills. On the third list write down your weaknesses.

There are two reasons for taking our weaknesses into consideration. In the first place, deep within ourselves we want most to succeed where we are weak. We want to turn our weaknesses into strengths. God understands this. The Holy Spirit seems to delight in calling us to tasks that seem too big for us, in order that his power and enabling may be manifest in our lives. If we let God transform weaknesses into strengths, after our goals are accomplished, we can sit back and marvel and even chuckle a little because we *know* we haven't done it; it has been God at work through us.

Secondly, as we write down weaknesses, we can take a good square look at them. We can ask ourselves why we think we can't do certain things. In many cases we are weak because someone has told us so often that we can't do a particular thing that we actually believe it. Have we ever *tried?*

In my younger years some friends and I were renovating some rooms. One of us was handy with the saw; she did all the carpentry. I drew up the decorating plans and made the slipcovers for the furniture. A third girl did the painting. I wanted to help her, but she steadfastly refused, saying I wouldn't do a good enough job. Instead I was assigned the task of sanding down all the dribble marks from previous paint jobs.

The conviction that I could not do a good job painting became so strong for me that it was not until many years later that I dared pick up a paint brush and try. I discovered, with joy, that with care and attention, I could paint.

So it is well to consider our weaknesses and ask if they are real or just figments of our imagination.

After these lists have been completed, share them with two or three friends. Ask them if they have any additions or corrections. Often we do not see ourselves as clearly as others see us.

Now go back and look over your list of prayer concerns or deeply cherished dreams and compare them with your lists of abilities, acquired skills and weaknesses. Can you see how they fit together?

3. *We do best cutting life into sizeable, manageable chunks.* To attempt too much only produces frustration and discouragement. Can you rank your concerns in order of the priority you want to give them? Next, considering the top two or three, write what you can *do* to meet these concerns or what you can *do* to begin to fulfill your dreams.

It is important to have a number of concerns or dreams or goals in mind even though you may pursue only one or two at a time. Why? Simply because the pursuit of a goal is often more fascinating and rewarding than the actual accomplishment of the goal. We need something to capture our enthusiasm as soon as a goal is won. Otherwise we are apt to experience a sag, even depression.

All the time, of course, you will be in a state of prayer and listening, asking God to check you if you are not moving according to his will.

If you are having difficulty setting goals because you feel no urgent, pressing concerns or because you really don't know what you would like to do, here is some practical counsel. Begin by doing whatever you find at hand waiting to be done. "Whatever your hand finds to do, do it with all your might," is a good rule to follow. If you can't see anything to do, go to your pastor or other church leaders, the principal of your local school, the local volunteer bureau, the mayor of your city or any philanthropic-minded leader of the community and ask if they have any openings where they can use you. Often as we become involved, we will find something that really grabs us.

4. *When you begin to get a sense of direction, talk it over with your family.* For you to work towards the fulfillment of your goals may cost them something. Are they happy with your projected plans?

5. *A life with goals usually means a narrowed-down and disciplined life.* You will have to weed out activities that have little or no meaning. You also will have to say 'no' to valid calls

for service. Are you prepared for this?

Once involved, don't be surprised when testings and discouragements attack you. They will only confirm your calling. If your motivation is God's call to you, the only thing that will really matter to you is your obedience. Don't be afraid of failure. You might not succeed in all your goals; you very likely won't. But at least you've had a good time trying, and what you have learned can help you attain your next goal.

6. *Every six months or so, review your goals.* Do you still consider them worthwhile? What progress have you made toward attaining them? Is it time to set new goals?

Always leave the door open for surprises God may have for you. You may be presented with an opportunity to serve or grow in areas about which you had never dreamed. In all your goal planning be open and flexible, ever ready for the Lord's direction.

Faithfulness in small responsibilities will lead to something bigger. Stretch and grow. It is thus you will continue to satisfy the need for adventure at the same time as you will be assuming more and more responsibility. You will discover that the years of midlife, rather than being aimless, drifting years, hold out the promise of the best years to come.

### My Covenant With God

My God, here am I.

By your grace I give you my all. I understand this to be my body, mind and soul, my faculties and abilities, my time and future, my home, goods, and money, my family and loved ones, my position and ambitions, my likes and dislikes, my habits, my failures, my sins, and all other things of any nature that I have counted my own.

I surrender this to your will and reckon it all from this moment on to be yours. Take me, cleanse me, and live out your life through me.

During my pilgrimage on this earth, I recognize that you have given me all these things as a trust, and I reckon myself to be a steward of them. I do this all to advance your kingdom and to bring a glory to your name. By your grace I shall rejoice to see this accomplished in whatever way you direct.

I direct my way unto you and trust you to lead me. I believe in you, I love you, and I trust you. I am confident that you are able to keep that which I have committed to you until I meet you face to face.

_____

(Signed)